The OTHER MAN

The
OTHER MAN

A Love Story

John F. Kennedy Jr., Carolyn Bessette, & Me

MICHAEL BERGIN

ReganBooks
An Imprint of HarperCollins*Publishers*

HarperCollins books may be purchased for educational, business, or sales promotional use. For information please write: Special Markets Department, HarperCollins Publishers Inc., 10 East 53rd Street, New York, NY 10022.

FIRST EDITION

Designed by Kris Tobiassen

Printed on acid-free paper

Library of Congress Cataloging-in-Publication Data

Bergin, Michael, 1969–
      The other man: a love story : John F. Kennedy Jr., Carolyn Bessette, and me / Michael Bergin.— 1st ed.
          p. cm.
      ISBN 0-06-072389-0 (alk. paper)
      1. Bergin, Michael, 1969– 2. Bergin, Michael, 1969—Relations with women. 3. Actors—United States—Biography. 4. Models (Persons)—United States—Biography. 5. Kennedy, Carolyn Bessette, 1966–1999—Relations with men. 6. Kennedy, John F. (John Fitzgerald), 1960– I. Title.

PN2287.B4344A3 2004
792.02'8'0929aB—dc22

                                                                                          2003067272

04 05 06 07 08 WBC/RRD 10 9 8 7 6 5 4 3 2 1

To Joy.
For her love, strength, and understanding,
especially during these difficult times.

To our son, Jesse.
For showing me the meaning of life.

And to our daughter, Alana Jade.
I can't wait to meet you.

I love you guys, from here to the moon and back.

But to see her was to love her,
Love but her, and love forever.
Had we never loved so kindly,
Had we never loved so blindly,
Never met—or never parted—
We had ne'er been brokenhearted.

—Robert Burns, "A Fond Kiss, and Then We Sever"

CONTENTS

1.

Crazy in Love

Thou art to me a delicious torment.
—Ralph Waldo Emerson

In the summer of 1992, at the age of twenty-three, I moved to New York City and went to work as a hotel doorman. This wasn't exactly the culmination of a lifelong dream. I'd gone to Manhattan to become a model, and, in fact, I'd been signed two years earlier by Click, one of the more reputable agencies. But other than occasional low-paying gigs, I wasn't making much progress, and I was beginning to wonder why I'd ever left Naugatuck, Connecticut. You'd be hard-pressed to find it on a map, but I'd been born and raised there, and my family still calls it home.

I missed them. And I missed small-town life. I barely knew a soul in New York. I was renting a room on the Upper East Side from a girl I'd met at the hotel, but that was already becoming something of a problem. She was lonely too, and she had managed to convince herself, misguidedly, that *I* was the answer.

New York is very tough on lonely people. When my shift ended at the Paramount Hotel, I'd walk fifty blocks from West Forty-sixth Street to the apartment in the East Nineties, and see all these happy couples on the street, arm in arm or hand in hand, smiling and cooing at each other, and I wondered when it was going to be my turn. I wanted to be happy too.

At night, I'd look at all the lit-up windows in the surrounding high-rises—*millions* of them—and I'd imagine all the happy people sitting down to dinner, watching a romantic movie on TV, then crawling into bed to make love for hours on end. When you're lonely, you tend to think you're the last lonely person in the world. You can't even imagine that there are other people out there— single people, couples, even married people—who are just as lonely as you are.

But they're out there, of course. They're everywhere. Some of them even stayed at the Paramount. There were women who would slip me their phone numbers when they tipped me, asking me to please call, they were available. And there were lonely men too. I remember one guest in particular, a man in his early forties, a regular: he always buzzed the front desk just as my shift was ending and asked the clerk to please send me up with the afternoon papers. It became something of a running joke at the hotel: "It's Michael's boyfriend again, pining for him." I'd go upstairs, newspapers in hand, and he'd open the door in the buff and ask me to come in.

"I can't," I'd say. "I'm sorry."

"Oh please, Michael. Just for a minute or two. You're so handsome."

"No," I'd repeat. "We're not allowed to fraternize with the guests, even on our own time."

And he'd look at me with those big puppy-dog eyes, like he was about to cry or something, and ask if I was sure. "I'll do anything, Michael. Anything at all. Just say the word. Tell me what you want. Spell it out."

To be honest, I felt kind of bad for the guy. I could relate to that kind of loneliness.

I was meeting people here and there, sure, but I couldn't afford to go out. And the problems with my roommate—I'll call her Sara—were only getting worse. She had taken to wandering around the apartment in nothing but sheer undies. She had a much nicer body than the lonely guy back at the hotel, and I was tempted, but I knew I'd only be asking for trouble. And I couldn't afford trouble—couldn't afford much of anything, in fact.

I didn't get much modeling work that fall, but I got promoted to bellhop. I wasn't sure how to take this. Did it mean I was finished as a model? That my future was in hotels?

One night I was feeling pretty low, so I went out for a beer with a struggling actress who worked the desk at the hotel. She was feeling pretty low herself, and we ended up in bed together, but the relationship didn't last. They usually don't when they're based on mutual despair, I guess. But it went beyond that: she had a snore like a foghorn, and it kept me up all night. I needed my beauty sleep, especially if I had any hope at all of making it in the modeling business.

She wasn't exactly thrilled about getting dumped, and every time I walked past the front desk she gave me the evil eye. I kept thinking about quitting the job, but I wasn't getting more than an hour's work here and there as a model, and I couldn't leave—not yet, anyway. So I scraped by. Day after day. Hoping for the big break and hustling off to one cattle call after another with the rest of the wannabe models in New York City.

Then it was back to the big glass doors at the Paramount Hotel.

"Welcome to the Paramount, Ms. Dunn." "Have a nice evening, Mrs. Freedman." "We've missed you, Mr. Goddard."

One day, en route to yet another casting call, I saw a fellow model on the subway. We both had our portfolios under our arms, clearly going to the same place. We half smiled, shrugged at each other, and got to talking. As it turned out, he was also repped by

Click. When the subway reached the station, we walked over to the audition together.

Keith, as I'll call him, was making ends meet as a waiter at an Upper East Side bar called Joe's Café. His brother, who I'll call Jason, worked there too, tending bar. Keith gave me his phone number and told me to come by the bar for a drink that night. It sounded like a couple of free beers were possible, so I agreed.

We reached our cattle call and walked into the lobby. It was full of good-looking men, milling around with their portfolios under their arms, smiling to beat the band, and trying hard not to look overly desperate. I was as desperate as the next guy, smiling just as hard. But it didn't help. I didn't get the job.

I went to Joe's Café that night. It was small and smoky and pleasant and full of pleasant-looking people. It even had a little dance floor. Several couples were shuffling around, hanging on to each other, looking very much in love. The place felt like the version of New York City I'd been looking for. Friendly. Warm. Intimate. Full of *promise*.

Keith was happy to see me. He hurried over, shook my hand, and introduced me to Jason. I sat at the bar and had a beer. There were some very attractive women in the place, and Jason went out of his way to introduce me to several of them. I was feeling good—better than I had in weeks. Before long, I had a nice buzz going, pretty girls were smiling at me, and Jason kept the free beer coming. I thought, *Here I am, where I belong.* I honestly felt as if I'd finally arrived. It might have been the beer, but then again, there was something about all the friendly faces in this tiny little Upper East Side bar that gave me hope.

"Do you party?" It was one of the pretty girls I'd been introduced to.

"Sure," I said. I thought she was inviting me to dance. I smiled and raised my bottle, toasting her. "I party. I *love* to party. My friends call me *Mr. Party*."

She led me off, past the small dance floor and down a dark corridor. I found myself in the storage room, with Keith and several other patrons. They were hunched over a small mirror, doing lines of cocaine. I'd seen enough movies to know what it was, but blow had never found its way to Naugatuck—at least not the Naugatuck I knew. I was pretty nervous, to be honest. I mean, a few minutes ago, I'd been sitting at the bar, enjoying my beer buzz, and thinking pleasant thoughts about all these pleasant people. And here they were, doing drugs. Such *nice* people too. Maybe drugs weren't as bad as I'd heard.

"Michael, have a snort." It was Keith. He was holding the mirror toward me in his left hand. There were two squiggly lines of cocaine on the surface, chopped to a fine dust, and a rolled-up dollar bill parked next to them.

"I, uh, I've never done this before," I said.

Everyone turned to look at me, but not in a judgmental way. They were real sweet about it. They all wanted to teach me how to do it. They were helpful in the extreme.

I took the rolled-up dollar bill, leaned over the mirror, and inhaled a line of coke. It was strangely electrifying. And *fast*. I was suddenly grinning like an idiot.

"How's that feel?" one of the girls asked me.

"Not bad," I said. I couldn't stop grinning.

Keith laughed. "You've got another line coming," he said.

I leaned over the mirror and repeated the procedure. *Whoosh!* What a kick.

One of the girls took the small mirror from my hand and ran her forefinger over the remaining coke. "Open your mouth," she said, moving closer. I opened my mouth. She rubbed her finger along my gums and teeth. Everything went numb and tingly. I liked the feeling. I grinned harder. I felt as if I'd just lost my virginity. I felt great. I felt *beyond* great. I was flying. I loved my newfound friends.

I decided to go back for more the following night, a Thursday. Sara got home while I was dressing. "Where you going?" she asked.

"To Joe's. This little club up the street."

"Can I come?"

"Sure," I said, not wanting to be a prick. "I'll wait."

"What's up?" she said on the way to the bar. "You seem different."

"Nothing," I said. "I'm in a good mood." And I *was* in a good mood. Suddenly I liked New York. My agency had called earlier in the day to say it still believed in me, and I was finally beginning to make friends: friends with recreational drugs.

We walked into Joe's and I introduced Sara to Keith and Jason, and some of the people I'd met the night before. Jason comped us a couple of drinks and we took a seat at the bar. I turned and noticed two women on the dance floor. The one who caught my eye was a tall, willowy blonde. She was dressed in black from head to toe, looking very elegant. She was dancing with her girlfriend, chatting, smiling. I liked the way she moved. I liked the way her long hair sparkled against her black dress.

"Who's that?" Sara asked. She had noticed me staring. I had completely forgotten that Sara was sitting next to me. I had forgotten everything but the willowy blonde.

"I don't know," I said. But I knew I wanted to know. And so did every other guy in the place: they couldn't keep their eyes off her.

When the music ended, the blonde approached the bar and said something to Jason that made him laugh. There was an easy familiarity there. I got the impression that they were more than friends. She looked up, saw me staring, and smiled. She was even more beautiful up close. I felt a real pull from her. I'd never been too good about approaching women in bars—I'm pretty shy, to be honest—but I told myself I wouldn't leave the bar without talking to her.

I had another beer and Sara asked me to dance. I begged off. I kept eyeing the blonde, and she glanced over at me from time to time. Sara was beginning to get irritated, but I couldn't help myself. I *needed* to talk to this girl. I was actually beginning to feel a little desperate. It was getting late and I didn't want her to slip away.

She returned to the bar and again said something to Jason. It was clearer than ever that these two had something going on. This only complicated matters. But someone down at the far end of the bar hollered for Jason, and when he moved off, I braced myself and went over.

"Hi," I said. "I'm Michael." I sounded like a dork. "I couldn't help noticing you."

She smiled back. "Carolyn," she said.

Suddenly Jason was back. And Sara was calling my name. *Loudly*.

"Michael!"

I looked over at Sara and waved—*I'll be right there!*—then turned back just as Carolyn moved off to rejoin her girlfriend. Shit. That was it? That was my big line? *I couldn't help noticing you.*

I found a book of matches at the bar, borrowed a pen, and scribbled my name and phone number on the inside flap. Carolyn was standing at the edge of the dance floor with her girlfriend, just then reaching for a cigarette. I hurried over with my book of matches and lit it for her. She leaned close. In the sudden glare she saw that I'd written my name and number on the flap. She blew out the match. I offered her the booklet, and she took it.

"Thanks," she said. And she and her girlfriend moved out onto the dance floor.

I didn't know how to read that. I walked back to the bar, where Sara was waiting. "Let's go," she said, pissed.

I didn't want to go, but it was late, and I didn't think she should walk home alone. I grabbed my jacket and followed her to the door, turning one last time for a look at the blonde. All I could think was, *If there's a God, she'll call.*

But she didn't call. Not the next day. Or the day after that.

I went back to Joe's on Saturday, hoping to run into her. She wasn't there. I paid a visit to the storage room and did a few lines. I was so wired that no one could shut me up. It was quite the transformation: in a few easy snorts, I'd gone from Monosyllabic Michael to Chatty Cathy.

I returned to the bar and drank and smoked and fidgeted and kept glancing toward the door, hoping Carolyn would appear, thinking perhaps I could *will* her to appear. It didn't work. I went home, feeling lousy. Part of it was Carolyn, of course, but part of it was the coke. Getting high was nice, but crashing was a total drag. I really didn't like the feeling. And I liked it even less the next morning. I couldn't shake the nausea. I didn't like the way I looked either. Black bags under bloodshot eyes.

Sunday I went back to Joe's and prayed, but Carolyn didn't show. I got invited out back for a line and tried to find the wherewithal to pass, but I figured a line or two wouldn't hurt.

It hurt. Monday I went to work feeling queasy and weak. The glass doors seemed heavier than ever. A couple of my colleagues asked if I was feeling all right. "Sure," I told them—but clearly I wasn't. It occurred to me that I didn't have the constitution for drugs and promised myself I'd never do them again. Then I thought about it and reconsidered: I might *dabble* now and then, but more carefully.

I returned to the apartment that night, looking forward to passing out on my red futon, but Sara was waiting for me—in a skimpy little tank top—and she was in a curious mood. She had that look on her face: *we need to talk.*

"What's up?" I asked.

"I'm glad you asked," she said. "I want to know what's going on between us."

"I don't know what you mean," I said.

"I want to know where this relationship is going."

I was a little taken aback. *Relationship?* That was a pretty loaded word. She was my roommate, I'd seen her in her underwear from time to time, and she was certainly easy on the eyes. But that was all there was to it. I never had any interest in getting involved, and I'd always been up-front about it.

"Sara," I said. "I don't think we have a relationship. I'm renting a room from you."

"Well," she said, "I have feelings for you. And I think you know it. And I think you're taking advantage of me."

Then we got into this whole thing about how I was paying only four hundred dollars a month, and how she—or, more accurately, her daddy—was saddled with the lion's share of the rent, and how she didn't think this was working out.

I was exhausted, and I didn't want to talk about it, to be honest. But suddenly the phone rang. I perked up, crossed the room, and grabbed it. I was hoping it was Carolyn. But of course it wasn't. It was somebody trying to sell me insurance. I hung up, visibly disappointed.

"What's the matter?" Sara said with a vicious look in her eye. "Your little girlfriend not calling?"

Bitch. I guess she'd seen me slip Carolyn my number.

"You're right," I said. "This isn't working out. I'll start looking for a new place to live."

"Try to make it fast," she said.

Super bitch.

★ ★ ★

The following day, a Tuesday, midafternoon, I got home to a ringing phone. I didn't hurry. I'd given up hope.

"Hello?"

"Michael?" she said. "Is this Michael Bergin?"

"It is," I said. I tried to keep the excitement out of my voice, but I'm not sure I succeeded.

"This is Carolyn," she said. "Carolyn Bessette. We met at Joe's."

"I remember," I said. I couldn't believe it. She had waited five days. Two I could understand, but *five*? "You really like to make a guy wait, don't you?" I said.

"Yeah," she laughed. "I figured I'd torture you a little."

"Well, you succeeded."

"You forgive me?" she asked.

"I'll think about it," I said.

"What are you doing tomorrow night?" she asked. Just like that: *What are you doing tomorrow night?* And wouldn't you know? I was free.

She lived downtown, on Second Avenue between Tenth and Eleventh, but she didn't mind the trip to my neck of the woods. I was waiting for her at the corner of Ninety-second and York when she arrived in a cab.

She stepped out and looked even more beautiful than I remembered. That lustrous hair, the shockingly blue eyes, those lips.

"Hey," she said, as if she'd known me for years. She began to walk and I fell into step beside her.

"Where're we going?" I asked.

"There are lots of little places around here," she said.

She walked fast. It was hard to keep up. She was *gliding*. We found a little sports bar a couple of blocks away and she led the way inside to a pair of high chairs at a small, round table. The waitress brought us a couple of beers and moved off.

Carolyn looked at me and smiled. "So," she said. "Who are you?"

She asked me a lot of questions. Where was I from? What was I doing in New York? How long had I been there? Was I liking it? Who was that girl she'd seen with me at Joe's Café?

I answered the best I could, but I didn't get much out of her, alas. I tried, but all she shared with me was that she was from Connecticut, like me, and that she worked as a publicist for Calvin Klein. Every time I pressed her for more details, she turned the conversation around and made it about *me*. I found it both unnerving and unusual, but not in a bad way. Most people are so hopelessly self-absorbed that they never tire of talking about themselves. Not Carolyn. She seemed genuinely interested in me. If I was going to get to know anything about her, it wasn't going to be that night.

She was unusual in another way too. She was very affectionate on that first date: very touchy-feely. She kept reaching for me across the table. For my hands, my wrists, my arms. She traced the veins on my forearm with the tips of her fingers. At one point I found her bare foot on my lap. I had no idea how it got there, but I began to massage it.

She looked across at me and smiled. Her whole face lit up when she smiled. I thought, *I could look at that face for the rest of my life.* I didn't even know her, but I felt connected to her in ways I couldn't begin to understand.

Then we were done with our beers, and it was time to go. She said she was busy and had a business dinner. I didn't want to leave without her number, and she gave it to me. Outside, I flagged a cab for her and she gave me a quick peck on the cheek and got in. I gave the driver twenty dollars and watched the cab until it rounded the corner.

I wanted her. I had a feeling she wanted me too. I called her the minute I got back to my apartment even though I knew she wouldn't be there. Her machine was on, so I left a short message. "I was going to wait five days to call you too," I said, "but I decided against it. You free tomorrow night?"

She came over the next night. It was a Thursday, and Sara was out on Long Island, visiting her parents, and doubtless complaining about me. We had the whole place to ourselves, but we didn't need the whole place. All we needed was the red futon. We walked through the door, straight into my room, and began kissing and taking off each other's clothes.

It was perfect. We were perfect together. It went beyond chemistry, beyond the way our bodies fit together, and beyond the way we responded to each other's touch. It was as if we were built for making love to each other. We were tender with each other. And very patient. We didn't want to rush this. It was too good. We wanted to savor every moment.

"Carolyn," I whispered, checking to see if she was still awake. She was wrapped around me, holding on for dear life.

"What?" she whispered back.

"I think I kind of like you," I said.

"I think I kind of like you too," she said.

And we drifted off to sleep.

In the morning, she clung to me until it was time to go. Then she leapt out of bed, hopped in the shower, and got dressed, all in about seven minutes flat. A simple dress, simple shoes, the tiniest hint of makeup—everything about her was pared down. She wasn't about noise or flash. She was about beautifully understated elegance.

"You are one gorgeous woman," I said. I couldn't stop staring at her.

"Thank you," she said, smiling. And then she was gone.

★   ★   ★

She had very full days at Calvin Klein. She had worked for the company in Boston, in sales, and Calvin himself had asked her move to New York and help run the publicity department. Before that, she'd gone to Boston University and graduated with a degree in education. But she decided not to pursue education. She went to work for the marketing department of a Boston nightclub.

See that? I'd been plying her with questions. I was going to get the Carolyn Bessette story out of her one way or another.

Despite her busy schedule, she came back that night. Late, after another business dinner. And then Friday, Saturday, Sunday. She was on my red futon four nights running. I was in heaven.

On Monday, we woke up, clinging to each other. I told her we had to make other plans that night because my hostile roommate was due back.

"We'll think of something," she said, and off she went.

I lay back down on the bed. I could smell her on the sheets. I *inhaled* her. She was partial to Egyptian Musk, an inexpensive perfume that smelled like fresh spices, and I could almost taste it on the pillows. Then I too got up, showered, slipped into my uniform, and went off to my intellectually challenging job at the Paramount Hotel.

She came to see me on her lunch break that very day. I felt awkward, opening the door for her, not knowing how I was supposed to greet her. A hug? A kiss? But Carolyn kept her distance. Unlike our first date, on this occasion she was very reserved in public, which I would learn was more her style.

"I just came by to say hello," she said, and before she could say more I had to run off to tend to an arriving guest.

Later, when I got a short break, we ran around the corner for a quick bite. Before we made it to the hot dog stand, she grabbed my hand and pulled me into an alley—where no one could see us—and kissed me hard.

"Meow," she said.

"I can't get enough of you either," I said.

We hooked up for a movie that night, and it was a pretty good movie. But we left after twenty minutes and went back to her place and made love. She may have been reserved in public, but in private she was intensely passionate.

Two days later she called and asked me to meet her at her place on her lunch break. I went over and she opened the door and we immediately went to bed. Afterward she began to cry.

"What's wrong?" I asked.

"Nothing," she said. "I'm very happy. *Too* happy."

"Me too," I said, drying her tears.

I loved the freckles on her nose. I loved the way they glowed whenever she blushed.

Friday I was back at her place. It was a nice building, a doorman building, but the apartment was unbelievably small—even by New York standards. As you entered, there was a microscopic kitchen to the right, a bathroom to the left, and the rest of the place—maybe ten or twelve square feet—was home. There was a box spring and mattress pressed up against one wall, and a closet just beyond that didn't even begin to hold her clothes. There were clothes every-where. Skirts, shoes, shirts, dresses, sweaters. *Mountains* of clothes.

There were picture frames on the walls, but none of them had any pictures in them—just gorgeous, ornate, empty frames. There was something a little eerie about them, ghostly even, and they added to the mystery. What was it about Carolyn that made her so cautious about revealing herself? Why did she never volunteer any-thing? Why did I have to fight for every tiny shred of information?

"I just don't like talking about myself," she told me once, when pressed. "I'm not that interesting. I'm just an ordinary girl."

Sure. On paper. But we're all pretty ordinary on paper. The story on Carolyn goes something like this: She was born in 1966 in White Plains, New York. She had twin sisters, Lauren and Lisa, who were a little older than she. Her parents, Ann and William, divorced in 1974, when Carolyn was eight, and her mother took the three girls and moved to Greenwich, Connecticut, where she worked for the public school system. She later married Richard Freeman, an orthopedic surgeon, and the family eventually settled in New Canaan.

Carolyn graduated from St. Mary's High School in 1984, where she was dubbed "the Ultimate Beautiful Person." After college and a brief stint with that nightclub, she found her way to Calvin Klein, in New York, where she worked briefly as a personal shopper to celebrity clients before Calvin himself tapped her for a job in his publicity department.

When I pressed her to explain how that had come about, she told me that Calvin had simply liked her sense of style. So did I. I didn't know a damn thing about style, but I knew she had it. And so did everyone else, it seemed. Whenever we were out together, people would notice her. They'd notice her in a pair of jeans and sneakers, and they'd notice her in Yohji Yamamotos and Manolo Blahniks. Men wanted her, women wanted to *be* her, and *I* had her. Me, a kid from the sticks in Connecticut. Twenty-three years old. What did this classy, sophisticated twenty-six-year-old see in me? Five feet and ten inches of pared-down elegance, so beautiful, so worldly, so refined, and she wanted *me*.

"This has got to go," she said.

It was barely ten days into the relationship, and she was already over at my place, going through my things. The object in question was a brightly colored short-sleeved shirt. "If you ever wear this again," she said, "I'll stop talking to you."

She was joking, of course, but not entirely. She took me shopping and had me run my hands over two almost identical T-shirts to show me which of them was superior. She taught me all about clothes: fabrics, styles, patterns, comfort—everything.

She bought me night creams. ("All the boys use them, no matter what they say.") She made suggestions about my hair, and told me what shampoos to use.

She even helped me with my diction, but she did it with such gentleness and such generosity of spirit that I was never embarrassed. "Try not to drop your word endings," she said. "It makes your sentences sound unfinished."

She was right. *Doin'. Sayin'. Goin'.* I sounded like a small-town hood, and Carolyn was trying to help me change that. She was educating me. Shaping me. *Refining* me. And I not only allowed it, I appreciated it.

"Why are you so good to me?" I said after a day of shopping and etiquette lessons.

"I'm not good to you," she said. "I just want the best for you. You deserve it."

Maybe, but she also wanted *me,* and I couldn't for the life of me figure out why. And this wasn't just false modesty. I meant it. What could she possibly see in me? I was a kid, uncultured in the extreme. I didn't know the first thing about art or music or literature or film, and I'd only just vaguely heard of Andy Warhol. Hell, I didn't even know how to *speak* properly.

"What can I say?" she joked. "Love is blind."

And private.

We seldom went out on actual dates together. She said she wasn't interested in making the scene and that she wanted me all to herself. So we spent a lot of time in bed together. In fact, in the first three weeks of our relationship—which, by the way, Carolyn never defined as a relationship—we were in bed together every single night. I wasn't complaining, but pretty soon her friends began to call. *We don't see you anymore. Where are you hiding? Where do you go at night? Where have you been?*

So we went to Joe's Café one Saturday. Separately. I got there at eight; she arrived an hour later. It was very friendly, very surface. Keith and Jason and the others were all there, and Carolyn paid no more attention to me than she paid to them. It struck me that she never kissed me in public, that she never held my hand in public, that she never so much as touched me if anyone she knew might be around. I felt as if she didn't want people to know about us—as if she wanted everyone to think we were just friends—but I decided to live with it. Carolyn had already made it clear that she preferred to keep her personal business to herself. And who was I to argue with her? Plus, she more than made up for it when we were alone together. She made me feel more wanted than I'd ever felt in my life.

There was only one person she actually introduced me to during this entire period, and that was her girlfriend Jules, who often crashed at her tiny apartment. One evening we ran into Jules on the street in front of Carolyn's place. "This is Michael," Carolyn said. "A friend of mine." I couldn't help but notice Carolyn's discomfort. It was almost as if she were telling her, *Don't read anything into this. There's nothing here.* Eventually she dropped the charade, however, and let Jules in on the true nature of our relationship. But Jules was the only one.

Did I find it odd? Yes, a little. But I accepted it. Because we were together every night. I loved the way she purred as she drifted off to sleep. I loved the way her warm breath felt against my neck. I loved the way she clung to me throughout the night. She never gave me any room in bed. I always found myself teetering on the edge of the mattress, with Carolyn pressed tight against me, and from time to time I'd have to get up and walk over to the other side. It didn't make any difference though. Within minutes, Carolyn, still asleep, would come searching for me and take me over that edge too.

I always woke up tired but happy. I couldn't believe my luck. Not all that long ago, I'd been the loneliest small-town kid in New York City. Now I was head-over-heels in love with the most fantastic woman in the world.

On weekends we'd go down to SoHo, look at all the tourists, window-shop. Or we'd saunter over to the flea market and see if there was anything that caught her eye. When I was hungry, we'd find a place to eat. Any little place would do. Carolyn had an odd relationship with food. She never thought about it, and she often forgot to eat. But when the food arrived, she could put it away like a regular truck driver. She'd eat what was in front of her, then turn her attention to my plate. And she always ate with her hands. She had this sort of hunt-and-peck technique: she'd push things around with her fingers and take what she wanted, but she did it with such grace and style that she was able to pull it off. She literally oozed class. She made it look as if eating with her fingers was something she'd studied in finishing school.

If she was still hungry after an entire meal of her own and half of mine—and, amazingly enough, sometimes she was—she'd order mashed potatoes and gravy. It didn't matter where we were. Could be KFC, could be the trendy Odeon. Mashed potatoes were mashed potatoes, and she loved them.

She had a weird relationship with beverages too. She could guzzle an entire bottle of Evian—a large one—in twenty seconds flat. Then she'd order a Snapple iced tea and work on that and one more after it.

She stored food and liquid for long periods of time; the city was her desert. I called her the Camel. She behaved as if she didn't know where her next meal was coming from, and the approach worked for her. She looked absolutely fantastic. She had a perfect, womanly body, perfectly proportioned, and she never exercised, not a day in her life. I had to kill myself to stay in shape—sometimes I'd run all the way back to my apartment from her place, and do four hundred crunches when I got there—but Carolyn was an enemy of exercise.

"I don't get it," she said. "What's the point?"

Weekday mornings were different; they were always something of a rush. Carolyn would lie in bed next to me, waiting until the last possible moment to get up, then she'd leap to her feet like a whirling dervish and shower and dress and fix her hair in her usual seven minutes flat.

If we had time, we'd stop at the little grocery store downstairs for a bagel. She always had the same thing: an everything bagel with all the dough scooped out, smothered in fresh tomatoes. No butter, no cream cheese: nothing but that hollow bagel and those juicy tomatoes.

She'd inhale it and ask me to walk her to the subway—yes, she actually took the subway from time to time, even though she loved taxis so much she called herself the Queen of Cabs—and she always walked fast. I had trouble keeping up.

"Come on, slowpoke!" she'd say. "I'm going to be late for work."

When we got to the subway entrance, she'd flash that smile of hers, wave good-bye, and off she'd go. No kiss. Nothing. No public displays of affection. As far as she was concerned, public displays of any kind were unseemly.

I'd watch her make her way down the stairs until she was out of sight, then I'd go back to the Upper East Side and get ready for my own day at the Paramount Hotel.

One weekday morning in late August, as we were rushing along, heading for the subway, cutting it close as usual, someone called out her name. "Carolyn!"

We turned and looked. It was John F. Kennedy Jr., cruising past on his bicycle. Carolyn waved back and the bike turned right at the light and John Jr. disappeared from view.

"Was that who I think it was?" I asked.

"Yes," she said.

"How do you know him?" I asked.

Carolyn didn't seem eager to tell me, but I pulled it out of her. She had been introduced to him at a charity event, by Kelly Klein, if I remember correctly, and later met him in a more professional capacity, when he came by the CK offices to try on clothes. The rich don't shop like you and me: they really *are* different. They're whisked off to private rooms where they're plied with champagne and caviar, and made to feel loved and magnificent. And Carolyn had been there to make sure that JFK Jr. felt loved and magnificent. It was part of her job at the time. She was dealing with all aspects of publicity—newspapers, magazines, the twice yearly fashion shows— and celebrity clients were very much part of the publicity machine. So, yes, other people brought the clothes for him, but Carolyn was there to make sure they did it well. They had to fawn, of course, but they weren't supposed to overdo it. She wanted to make sure that JFK Jr. had only good things to say about his shopping experience when he got back to his close personal friends Calvin and Kelly Klein.

By the way, that was how they met. There was a story making the rounds—and it made the rounds for years and years—that they had met jogging in Central Park. But it was untrue. They first met, briefly, at that charity event, then again in that suitelike dressing room. And Carolyn assured me that she'd been underimpressed.

But John Jr. called. And called. And called.

"He was incredibly persistent," she told me as we continued on our way to the subway.

"What happened?" I asked.

"Nothing," she said. "We went out a couple of times."

"Dinner?"

"Dinner," she repeated. "And once or twice to Martha's Vineyard."

"You went to Martha's Vineyard with John Kennedy Jr.?" I wasn't exactly thrilled by the idea. Not that I suffer from retroactive jealousy, but I was nuts about Carolyn and didn't want anything to go wrong.

We were at the entrance to the subway now. She put her hand on my arm, as if to reassure me. "It was nothing, Michael."

"Nothing," I said, trying to control my voice. "You don't go away for a weekend with a guy and say it's nothing."

"It really was nothing," she said, with a note of irritation now. "I went as a friend."

"What does that mean, *friend*?" It occurred to me that she had never once admitted to any kind of serious liaison with any man. Not Jason. Not JFK Jr. Not the hockey player she had dated in college. It was almost as if she didn't want to acknowledge that she had any sexual history at all. She wanted to be a virgin for me. Every other man in her life had been just a *friend*.

"Michael," she said. "Let's drop this. Nothing happened. It was no big deal. You have nothing to worry about."

And then she turned and hurried down the stairs to the subway.

I walked off, worrying. I didn't know why I felt so insecure. Despite my small-town-kid misgivings, I knew Carolyn was in love with me. It wasn't that she told me so; it was more about the way she held me, the way she looked at me.

Still, I thought it was unreasonable of her to deny that she had a past. It didn't make her less pure. It didn't make her a bad girl. We all have pasts. But a past with JFK Jr.? Well, that was a little troubling. If the roles had been reversed—had it been Madonna gliding past on roller skates, waving at me, and I said, "Oh, it was nothing. We went on a cruise to Mykonos one long-ago weekend"—I wonder how Carolyn would have responded.

I called at her at work later that morning. "Are you sure nothing happened?" I said. My insecurity was showing, but I didn't give a damn.

"Michael," she said, her voice clear and firm. "Nothing happened. And I really don't want to talk about it. People tell each other too much about their pasts. I have nothing to hide. I just don't think talking about the past does anything for anyone."

Maybe she was right. Maybe people *did* share too many details. I'd been in love with a girl I met in high school, who I'll refer to as Rachel, and I'd shared that with Carolyn. But only fleetingly. With few details. So I followed her lead and let it drop. She was the worldly one; she was the sophisticate in the relationship. I really didn't need to share *everything*. I didn't need to tell her about the other girls I'd been with. What was the point? Similarly, if she didn't want to talk about JFK Jr., she shouldn't feel any pressure to do so. I was curious, sure, and I wanted to know. But at the end of the day, was it really my business? And what was the point? So I decided then and there that I wasn't going to press her. I was going to live in the present. I was going to enjoy the moment.

She called me back later that morning and asked if I was free for lunch. Maybe she was trying to reassure me. I don't know. I just know it worried me more; it made me feel even less secure. *Why is she trying to reassure me if I have nothing to worry about?* Jesus, the male mind at work!

I went off to meet her for lunch, still thinking about John Jr. He was American Royalty. A woman like Carolyn deserved a man like him. It was hopeless. Who was I kidding? Real Love only happens in the movies. Maybe she was meeting me for lunch to dump me.

And then I saw her coming down the street; I saw her before she saw me. And when she looked up and spotted me, she did this crazy double take. Like, *Who are you?* She looked lit from within; she looked *that* happy to see me. And in that instant all the doubts I had about our future were magically dispelled.

And this time she actually kissed me smack on the lips, right there in the middle of the sidewalk, in the middle of the city. A genuine public display of affection. And I remember thinking, *This is the girl I'm going to marry. I don't doubt it for a second. This woman here is going to be my wife.*

So we hurried through lunch—she wolfed down her meal and devoured half of mine—and managed to avoid any mention of John Jr. She talked about work, an upcoming fashion show, and about a new designer. And then she had to run. "I'll call you later," she said, adding, "if I have time."

"Can't we get together for dinner?" I asked.

"I don't know," she said. "I'll let you know."

And she was off. My gorgeous Carolyn. Carolyn, who liked talking about the future even less than she liked talking about the past, if that was remotely possible. Even the near-term was too complicated for her. She refused to make a plan. It always depended on how things went at work, how much she got done, whether she had to go to that boring thing at the Met.

But I didn't mind. I was idiotically happy. As far as I was concerned, it was nothing short of a miracle that I had this amazing woman in my life.

I got home walking on air, and a phone call from Click sent me into the clouds. The agency had booked me for a gig Saturday afternoon. They needed a guy with nice abs for a couple of hours. Was I available? "Ten sharp. Be on time." So when Saturday rolled around, I went to the studio and introduced myself to one of the assistants and she hollered in the direction of main room, "The abs are here!" And I guess that's what I was: a set of abs. And they lit the abs and shot the abs and sent the abs on their way. The photographer didn't look at my face once. I was humiliated.

I told Carolyn about it that night, and she said that was the nature of the business. "These people aren't interested in getting to know you," she said. "It's about getting what they need from you; it's about the work. Don't take it personally."

In a way, that was very helpful. She took a look at my portfolio and was incredibly encouraging. There wasn't a lot there, she said, but what I had was very good. "I see that gorgeous body on the side of a bus someday," she added. "And I really mean that. I wouldn't say that lightly."

She was very good that way. She was never afraid to compliment me or give me encouragement. I think it was a function of her own self-confidence. I'd been around women who put me down, made me feel bad, or said things to fuel my insecurity, as if I wasn't sufficiently insecure already, but being with Carolyn made me see that that was really about their own fears. People tear people down to keep them close—to make them feel so horrible and unwanted that they'll never leave. That's what emotional abuse is all about. Well, with Carolyn it was the exact opposite. She tried to build me up, make me feel good about myself and my future. She was working at giving me self-confidence, because she knew I didn't have much.

"You are stunningly handsome," she told me over and over again. "Don't you realize how handsome you are?"

Frankly, no, I didn't realize it. But Carolyn tried to make me believe it. She always noticed handsome men. She had a thing about beauty, I guess, in both men and women.

"Get the bill," she said one night in a restaurant. We hadn't finished eating, but she was ready to go, and she was devouring me with her eyes. "Take me home right now and make love to me or I'll scream."

How could I not be crazy about her?

And we *made love*. It wasn't about sex with us. It was lovemaking as I had never experienced it before.

Then again, I have to admit that I wasn't all that experienced, sexually speaking. I was still a kid—and a shy kid at that. I'd gotten off to a late start, and I remained awkward around women. I didn't know how to approach them, didn't know what to say. And if by some miracle I found myself in bed with any of them, I wasn't always sure where to start or what to do. Until I met Carolyn, I'd always been anxious around women. In Carolyn, I found what I was looking for, and I didn't want anyone else.

She was very comfortable with her body. She'd come to bed in nothing but a T-shirt and a thong, and slide up next to me, like a cat, coquettish, playful, enjoying the drama, pulling away with feigned shyness until I couldn't take it anymore.

I began to believe the fairy tales. You know: how we're all out there looking for our magical missing half. Well, Carolyn was my missing half. I knew it deep in my heart. I had misgivings about my job, my career, and my future, but I had no misgivings about Carolyn. Sure, there'd been that business with John Jr., but that was in the distant past. And nothing had happened, right? So maybe it nagged at me a little—*John F. Kennedy Jr.*—so what? I had it under control.

"Carolyn," I said one muggy night. We were at her place, trying to stay cool. "Are we boyfriend and girlfriend or what?" I felt like an idiot for saying it, but I guess I needed some reassurance.

Carolyn looked at me. "Why does it have to be like that?" she said gently. "Why do people feel a need to define things? We're together. Isn't that enough?"

She was right. It was enough. It's not like I had to pin her or anything. This was New York, after all. People did things differently in New York.

The next night, after we made love, she cried.

"What's wrong?" I asked.

"Nothing," she said, still crying. "Why are you doing this to me?"

"What am I doing to you?"

"This is too good," she said. "I'm too happy. I don't want this to end."

"Why should it end?" I said, wiping the tears from her face. "It doesn't have to end."

"Everything ends," she said, then she turned her back to me and drifted off to sleep.

In the morning, I asked her if she was all right. She acted as if the previous night had never happened. I found it a little scary. She was already late, so she skipped the bagel, flagged down a cab, and I jogged the many miles home, worrying the whole way.

Carolyn ran things in the relationship. You might say she had control issues. She called when she wanted to call and saw me when she wanted to see me. But so what? She called all the time, and we saw each other all the time. In fact, in the course of those first three weeks, we had spent all but one night together.

She was also very clingy. It went beyond the way she held on to me at night, stuck to my side like a magnet. I began to notice a hint of panic in her eyes whenever we parted ways. Once she called and couldn't reach me, and she worked herself into a frenzy.

"Where have you been?!" she said the next day, having finally tracked me down.

"Nowhere," I replied. "I was out jogging."

"You should let me know where you are in case I need you."

"Okay," I said. "I will. I'll try."

"That's not good enough."

So she had abandonment issues. A lot of people do. And hers were well founded. Her father left home when she was eight years old. Like half the population, she was raised by a single parent. And the rest of us, those who were raised in happy homes, don't we have issues too? I certainly did. And I was struggling with them at that very moment. What had Carolyn been crying about the night before? What was I doing to her that she didn't want to discuss? And if she didn't want to discuss it, what steps could I take to fix it?

I began to overanalyze things. I looked back over the past few days and convinced myself that—despite the clinginess—she seemed to have become somehow more removed, more distant. Half the day would go by and she wouldn't have called. I usually tried not to bother her at work, but that day was different—I was feeling anxious—and I called her several times. Various assistants took messages for me, and I left word, repeatedly, on her answering machine at home, but I didn't hear back from her until the following morning, a Friday.

"Sorry I didn't get back to you," she said. "I had a crazy day. Let's talk later. I'll call."

She didn't call. I tried repeatedly but couldn't get through. I left more messages on her machine, trying to keep the petulance out of my voice. Nothing. I called again before I went to sleep that night and she didn't answer. It was after one in the morning.

I slept fitfully. Who had abandonment issues now?

Around lunchtime, Carolyn showed up at the hotel. I was very glad she was there, but it was a Saturday, and I was pretty busy. Plus there was the humiliation to deal with: *Here's your sort-of boyfriend, Michael, opening and closing doors and smiling his most professional smile. Ain't he cool?*

Carolyn seemed to be getting impatient. I had to keep running off to greet guests and hustle bags and do my job. And I couldn't take any chances; I *needed* the job. It was the only thing keeping me off the streets.

The next time I broke away, stealing another moment with her, a very strange thing happened. Carolyn seemed downright angry. She was normally so patient and loving, and here she was, standing in the Paramount lobby, looking seriously pissed. I didn't get it.

"I'm sorry," I said. "I'm just really busy."

"Is that it?" she said with a snarl in her voice.

"What do you mean?" I asked.

"I don't think you're very happy to see me," she said. "You looked unhappy from the moment I showed up."

"Carolyn," I said, "that's not true, and you know it's not true. I couldn't be happier to see you. I wish I could run away with you right now. But I can't. I need this job."

"Great," she said, angrier than ever. And abruptly she walked past me and marched right out of the hotel. I was stunned. I'd never seen that side of her. I didn't understand it.

I called her the moment I got home. Her friend Jules answered the phone. "Carolyn's not here," she said.

I called back an hour later. Nothing. I called at midnight and left another message. Still nothing. I called the following afternoon, and Jules picked up and said she hadn't seen Carolyn since morning. And, yes, she had given her my messages; *all* of them.

Boy, I thought, *that was cold.*

I didn't know what to do. I didn't want to make a pest of myself, and I didn't want to make trouble for Carolyn, so I decided to stop calling. I told myself she'd call me as soon as she got through whatever it was she was going through. After all, it was pretty clear that I wanted to talk to her. I'd left at least a dozen messages.

Five days went by and still Carolyn didn't call. I phoned home. My mother sensed something was wrong, and I told her that I'd had a little tiff with Carolyn. She hadn't met Carolyn, but she'd heard about her from me, and I didn't know what more to say. Was I supposed to tell her that Carolyn had dumped me with no explanation whatsoever? That we had just spent an entire month together, both of us walking on air, unable to get enough of each other, and that she had suddenly changed her mind about me?

I thought back to that last time I'd seen her, a few days earlier, at the Paramount, and about how uncharacteristically harsh she'd been. I didn't understand what that had been about either. It felt as if she'd come to see me to pick a fight. Why? I was very confused.

I didn't hear from her the next day, or the day after that, and I finally got the hint.

The following weekend, I went home to lick my wounds.

2.

Home

I am two fools, I know, for loving, and for saying so.
—John Donne, Elegy 17, "The Expostulation"

I grew up in a three-bedroom, two-story home in Naugatuck, Connecticut, and that's where I went to recover. The house has a small but well-tended yard and one of those aboveground swimming pools you see in working-class neighborhoods across the country. Except for the bright blue siding, the house looks pretty much like any other house on the block: serviceable, solid, and solidly middle-class. The neighbors were decent, hardworking people: firefighters, schoolteachers, real estate agents, businessmen. And they all had kids of course, so it was a great place to grow up.

I was actually born in nearby Waterbury, on March 18, 1969, but when I was three months old my parents packed up and moved to Naugatuck, and they live there to this day. My father was a sergeant with the Connecticut state police. My mother was a hairstylist. I was the third of four children.

Going back to Naugatuck to visit was nothing unusual for me—I went home often; I love my family—but going home in this sorry state affected everyone. I was seriously unhappy, my heart was broken, but I didn't want to talk about it. I just wanted to be there, regressing, wallowing in my misery, with Mom and Dad close at hand.

My father, Ronald, has been the most influential force in my life. He's six-foot-one, with hazel-brown eyes, a small gap between his front teeth, and reddish hair that turned dark when he was still an infant. He was twenty-one when he married my mother, Lorraine, and they had three kids in quick succession. My brother, Ron Jr., my sister Tina, and me. Jessica came along many years later.

Dad worked narcotics and homicide for the state police. He was also a certified scuba diver, which meant he was called upon from time to time to look for murder weapons or pull dead bodies from the water. High-stress work, yes, but he never brought the stress home with him. When he walked through the door, he'd smile that gap-toothed smile and leave it all behind.

My mother is a close second in the influence department. She was the heart of our old-fashioned family. She was the moral center of the Bergin household. She tried to help us make sense of this crazy world, and she never tired of reminding us that actions had consequences. But even when we slipped up, she was always there to support us. "Nothing is more important than family," she'd say over and over again. She believed it too, as did my father. Both of them took parenting very seriously. Homework, meals, TV—we tried to do everything together as a family. Sports—same thing. Mom and Dad always did their best to make it to all our games, and they cheered louder than any of the other parents in the stands. That's the way it felt to me anyway. And I'll never forget it.

By the time I was eight years old, sports had pretty much taken over my life. I was on a Little League baseball team and played Little Pal basketball. I never missed a practice or a game. I loved playing and winning, but playing and losing wasn't so bad either. It was *not* play-ing I couldn't handle. I needed my fix.

I'll never forget one Saturday when I was eleven and my father was late coming home, and I almost missed basketball. I was stand-ing at the living room window, waiting for him, bawling my eyes out, thinking for sure the old man had forgotten. But then there he was, pulling up in his car, and off we went. I got to the court with an entire minute to spare. I scored twenty-six points that day—the most I'd ever scored in my life. I was ecstatic.

Of course, not everything was sports. I had other needs too. I was a normal kid, and normal kids like to make trouble from time to time. I broke a few streetlights in my day. I lobbed snowballs into passing cars and made crank calls every now and then. Sometimes, on hot summer nights, I'd camp out in a backyard tent with friends from the neighborhood. When the lights went out in their parents' room, we'd run off and explore Naugatuck After Dark. We'd toss eggs through windows. Ring doorbells. Hop from one neighbor-hood pool into the next—at two in the morning. But I lived with a cop, so how bad could I be?

I wasn't an angel, no. I even sassed my mom occassionally. I still remember the way she used to chase me around the house with a big wooden spaghetti spoon, trying to knock some sense into me. She never caught me, of course, but good sense crept up on me anyway.

By the time I reached middle school, I was actually learning to think for myself. Sort of. Plus, it didn't hurt that my father was a cop. I couldn't put anything past him. He'd look at me with those cop eyes and I'd all but beg him to hit me with a telephone book so I'd feel less guilty.

The fact is, my parents loved me, and I wanted to be worthy of their love. I wanted to make them proud. It may not sound like much, but it made all the difference in the world to me. I wasn't just a kid to them. I was a person, with my own needs and wants, and they respected that. I wanted to grow up to be just like my father. And I wanted to marry a girl just like my mom.

When I was nine years old, my parents had another child, a little girl, Jessica, and I loved taking care of her. I wasn't crazy about changing her diapers, but I learned to hold my breath for long periods of time and suffered through it. I loved carrying her around the house and showing her off to the neighbors, and I loved rocking her to sleep when she cried. I used to take her from her crib and put her in bed with me, pillows piled high all around the perimeter so that she wouldn't fall off. I knew early on that I wanted a big family of my own someday. I wanted kids and grandkids and more cousins than my kids could count, and I wanted to see all of them crowded around a big Thanksgiving table.

I had that growing up. We were a loud, extended family. My grandparents had a store in downtown Waterbury called International Foods, and my grandmother runs it to this day. My grandparents practically lived in the store. They were there sixteen, seventeen hours a day, and I went there every chance I got. These were my mother's parents, Peter and Angie. They were American born, but their parents had come over from Italy. The store smelled of olives and dried meats and herbs and imported cheeses. They made great sandwiches, and at lunchtime the lines would spill out onto the sidewalk. During the holidays you practically had to fight your way inside. My grandmother was also famous for her food baskets of cheeses, crackers, fruits, nuts, aromatic coffees, jams, and olive oils. During the Christmas rush, the whole family would be there helping out. It was like an assembly line, everyone clowning and hollering and tending to their assigned chores, with grandma quietly taking it all in. It was *Leave It to Beaver*, Italian-style, with a little hint of Irish. And that's what I think of when I think of family.

★ ★ ★

One chilly winter afternoon when I was thirteen, one of the neighbor-hood girls approached me and my friend John, as I'll call him. She was a year older than we were, and worldly in a trashy, small-town way. She just came right out and asked us if we'd ever been laid. We shook our heads no. She told us to come by later; we'd work something out.

So night fell and John and I hooked up, went over to her house, and found her waiting for us in the shadows of the yard. She took a bedsheet off her mother's clothesline, led us around the side of the house, and set it on the cold, damp grass. The wind was blowing, and I was shivering—and not just from the cold either.

John went first. I watched. When he was done, in about sixty earth-shaking seconds, I peeled off my pants, climbed on top of her, and started shivering harder. I parked myself between her legs and looked down at her, then I looked over at John. He was staring dead at me, grinning to beat the band. I guess he wanted to be entertained.

"What are you waiting for?" the girl said. She had an edge in her voice, and she just lay there, like a big, pasty log, staring up at me.

"It's cold," I whispered back.

"I'm giving you *this,* and you're complaining about the cold?"

"I'm sorry," I said. "It's not working."

It certainly wasn't. Any fool could see that.

She got up, put on her pants, and marched around the corner, back into her house. I groped in the shadows for my shoes and laced them up, and snuck off with John.

"Cool, huh?" he said, still grinning.

"I guess," I said, but I didn't really know. And I wasn't going to learn for a while: I remained a virgin for another four years.

Having had limited success in carnal matters, I poured myself into my studies. I went to City Hill Middle School, in Naugatuck, for three years, grades six through eight, and I was class valedictorian each time out. So I was a virgin, a jock, nervous around girls, and short for my age, but no matter: my parents were very proud of me.

"An education, son," my father said, "that's the most important thing in life."

I had heard different—I had heard sex was more important—but I was probably the most naive thirteen-year-old kid on the eastern seaboard. Yes, I had heard about masturbation too; and, yes, I'd woken up with an erection from time to time. But I'd never brought myself to orgasm. I didn't even know what an orgasm was.

Then I met this older girl, who I'll call Donna, who was fifteen. She must have had a thing about short, smart jocks because one day she borrowed her mother's car and took me for a drive. We parked at this place on the edge of town that was very popular with the sexually progressive crowd, and she knew how to use her mouth.

I didn't know what the hell was going on, as good as it felt, and when I came, I swooned and cried out in fear. "W-what happened?" I asked, looking down at that sticky mess.

"What do you mean?" Donna said.

"Is this normal?"

She studied me in disbelief as if to say, "Did you really just ask me that?" Then she lit a cigarette, started the car, and drove me home.

"Thanks," I said.

"You're welcome," she said.

I watched her drive off. I thought I should be feeling more manly somehow, but I wasn't feeling manly at all. This business of living was more complicated than it seemed.

For a few days, I walked around in a daze. I wanted to talk to someone about it, but I didn't think my mother would understand. I thought about my father, but I really didn't know how to broach the subject. So I went over to my grandparents' store. My grandfather didn't look so hot. When I got there, in the middle of the afternoon lull, my grandmother was busy laying out his heart medications—about a dozen multicolored pills. He smiled at me when I came through the door.

"How you doin', Mikey?" he said.

"Great, Grandpa," I said.

But I wasn't doing great. I was confused. I needed someone to explain the Meaning of Life to me, and he didn't exactly look like the right guy just then. He got up and cut me a slab of cheese. "An Italian blue. It's strong, but you'll love it," he said before going off to tease my grandmother.

For a while, I tried to put girls out of my mind. I focused on school and raked in the plaudits. Most Popular. Best Looking. Best Personality. Best Dressed. Teacher's Pet. I wanted to be liked, and I wanted to be popular, but life throws some curveballs at you, and my popularity ended up working against me—with the *guys,* anyway.

"Hey, Bergin, think you're pretty?"

"No, I don't," I said over and over, and I really meant it.

But they never listened. There was a group of guys who seemed intent on rearranging my features. And they went at it every chance they got.

One Saturday night I was in downtown Naugatuck with my friend Timmy Cousins and a couple of other kids from City Hill. We were working on a six-pack and standing around trying to look cool. Timmy was very hot for one of the girls there, and he kept hitting on her. She played along, liking the attention, until her ex-boyfriend showed up. Timmy was pretty big though, and the ex-boyfriend took one look at him and decided he wasn't going to bother trying. Instead, he looked over at me, smaller and less intimidating, and told me he was going to kick my ass.

"W-why?" I said. "What did I do?" I was already scared. The ex-boyfriend was the toughest kid in school, and I'd heard he was quick as lightning with his fists.

"You're tryin' to pick up my girl, that's what."

"No I'm not," I said. "Honest." I wanted to tell him that I didn't know the first thing about girls, but I didn't think it would help.

"We'll see about that," he said. Then he came close and whispered that he'd see me Monday, at school, bright and early. I guess he didn't want to beat me to a pulp in front of his girlfriend and show her his true colors.

I was terrified. I asked Timmy to help me out. He was only picking on me because I was an easier target. "You're the one that was messin' with his girl," I said.

"Ah, don't worry about it," Timmy said. "Fuckin' guy's all talk."

I worried all weekend. One terrifying thought kept playing in my head like a broken record: *I'm going to get my ass kicked.*

Monday morning I got off the bus, already shaking. He was standing by the front door with his gang of thugs, grinning at me. "How you doin', Mikey?" he said, all pleasant-like.

"Good," I said, my voice cracking. I kept walking.

"Enjoy it while you can," he said.

All morning, nothing happened. Afternoon, more of the same. School let out, still nothing. He was outside grinning at me like a gorilla. "See you around, Mikey," he said.

When I got home, I was so tense I couldn't eat. I was hoping that Timmy Cousins had been right—that this guy was all talk—but something in my gut told me I had a beating coming, and that this son of a bitch was only putting it off so he could watch me suffer.

"What's the matter with you?" my brother said.

"Nothin'," I said, looking across the dinner table at him. "I don't know what you mean."

"Sounds like you're praying under your breath," he said.

Next morning, same routine. Bus dropped me off and I made my worried way toward the school entrance. Mr. Son of a Bitch and his friends were waiting for me, and they asked me to join them behind the school.

I demurred. "I've got to get to class."

"I'm not going to ask you again."

"I don't want to be late."

Bam! His fist connected with my lip. Blood spurted everywhere. I looked up at him and a wall of his fleshy friends and got the message. I went.

When we were behind the school, safely out of sight, he said, "Don't ever go near my girl again."

"I never touched your girl," I said. "I swear it."

"Liar."

By this time a regular crowd had gathered—it felt as if every kid in school was there watching—so I was feeling both terrified and deeply humiliated.

"Look," I said, beginning to plead, but I never got a chance to finish the sentence.

Bam! He hit me again. Then he put up his dukes and started circling me like he was Sugar Ray Leonard or something.

"I didn't do nothin' to you," I said, whining a little. I really said that. That's the way we talked in Naugatuck. We weren't big on elocution. You could always tell the Naugatuck kids: they were the ones that had trouble with word endings: "I ain't screwin' around, man. Don't be messin' with me, smartass."

"You gonna fight or you gonna whine?" he asked me.

I opted for whining. "Why are you pickin' on me?" I said, and despite my best efforts I could feel tears welling in my eyes. "I don't even *like* your girl."

Bam! Bastard hit me in the chin.

By this time my face was so numb I hardly felt it at all, but I hurt in other, deeper ways. I had to fight the urge to break down and cry. It seemed like practically the whole school was there. It would've been the end of me.

I thought about trying to throw a punch, but in midthought he socked me in the head, and I stumbled backward, dazed. Suddenly the bell rang and everyone took off, leaving me there. I had never felt so alone. Where were my friends? Did I even have any friends?

Just then I looked up and saw one of the teachers hurrying across the yard. I began to cry. I tried to keep it inside, I wanted to be a man, but what the hell was the use?

"You all right?" the teacher asked, getting closer.

"No," I said. And I turned and hopped the fence and ran.

"Michael!" she shouted. "Michael Bergin, you come back here this instant!"

But I wasn't going back. No way was I going to face any of those kids. I was *never* going back.

After about a mile, I stopped running. But I kept walking. I decided to walk all the way home. It took me two hours to get there. When I stepped through the front door, my mother turned to look at me. "Michael! What are you doing here? What happened to your face? Is that blood on your shirt?"

And I just lost it. "What do you want from me?" I shouted. "Leave me alone!"

"Hey!" she said. "Let's show a little respect here."

She took me upstairs, cleaned me up, and got the whole sordid story out of me, then put me in the car and drove me right back to school. I whined all the way, but she wasn't hearing it. We marched into the principal's office, and she made me rat the guy out. He got a three-day suspension. Now I knew for sure I was dead. But three days later he came back and he didn't do a thing to me. I guess he figured two black eyes and a fat lip were enough: he'd made his point. I was free to get on with my miserable life.

Thank God for little miracles, right?

Shortly after I turned fifteen, I got a job as a dishwasher at the Waterbury Club, a members-only restaurant that catered mostly to doctors and lawyers. My father knew the manager, and my brother already worked there, so getting the job was a breeze. I spent close to a year in the kitchen, then joined my brother bussing tables, which was more fun than washing dishes. Plus, there were people around. I could talk to them and pass the time.

I stayed on that first summer, putting in more hours. And when the janitor went on vacation to Niagara Falls, I took over for him for two weeks. I spent my days mopping floors and swabbing toilets, and it didn't bother me a bit.

"Someday you'll look back on this and you'll be glad you did it," my mother said. "A man should never think he's too good for anything." I don't think she was saying that this was my destiny; I think she was saying that life throws some shit at you, and that you should always be prepared for it. It was more of that moral center, good value stuff I was telling you about, and it worked for me.

Sometimes I'd work at the club's four-lane bowling alley in the basement. It was duckpin bowling, with regular ten pins, but it wasn't automated. There was this little space between each alley, and I'd crouch low and wait for the ball to come barreling along. Then I'd sweep the fallen pins out of the way and hurry back and wait for the second ball to come roaring toward me. It was noisy and exhausting, and you never got more than a few seconds break at a time, but most of the members were pretty good tippers.

My brother and I were there one night in 1984, at closing time, when my father came by to pick us up.

"I have some bad news, boys," he said.

"What?" I asked.

"It's Grandpa," he told us, his voice just a notch above a whisper. "Grandpa passed away."

We didn't say a word. We got in the car and drove home, both my brother and I numb with shock. This was my first experience with death, and I was terrified. I kept thinking of my grandfather as a corpse. I imagined him being laid out in a casket, and it really scared me.

When we were about a minute from the house, my brother and I looked at each other and simultaneously burst into tears. I'm talking serious sobbing; I could hardly catch my breath. My father pulled over, turned toward us, and handed both of us tissues. He spoke a little bit about old age, death, and heaven, and he told us that God took everyone when their time came—even the people we loved most. I thought this was horribly unfair, and I didn't like it at all.

"Your grandfather was a wonderful man," my father told us. "He lived a good life. He couldn't have asked for better."

That was all well and good, but I loved my grandfather, and I already missed him. I couldn't imagine walking into the store and him not being there. I couldn't imagine Christmas without him. I couldn't imagine Thanksgiving without Grandpa at the table.

My mother was even more of a wreck than I was. It was *her* father, after all. He'd been there to bring her home from the hospital. He'd cooed at her when she was just a little baby. He'd helped her with her homework and dried her tears and walked down the aisle with her to give her away to my old man. That's what parents do, or should do anyway. Be there for you. Every step of the way. And now he was gone.

At the wake, I saw that unholy grief in her eyes. The way she looked down at his face for the last time. I wished I could take away her pain, but I didn't know where to begin. And then the guys came by after to close the casket and I knew it was really over. It felt so *final*. I was fifteen years old, and I didn't want to think about death or dying, but I had to think about it. I felt emptied out. Hollow. It would be more than a decade before I felt that kind of loss again, and—may my grandfather forgive me—it seemed even harder the second time around. That second time was on July 16, 1999, when Carolyn died, along with her sister Lauren, and her husband, John F. Kennedy Jr. But standing in the living room at that wake, I could never have imagined how my life would be touched by something like that.

The following year I went to Naugatuck High. Some of the same assholes from City Hill Middle School came along, of course, and I met all sorts of new assholes when I got there. My world was divided into the jocks, which was us, and the potheads, which was them. So of course the potheads didn't like me. Plus, I was short and their girlfriends were always flirting with me. And I was a bit of an apple-polisher, which didn't help. Are you getting the picture here? I didn't enjoy that first year.

But the summer after my freshman year changed everything: that was the summer I fell in love for the first time in my life.

A new roller-skating rink had just opened in downtown Naugatuck, and I was there every Friday night. One night I saw this petite brunette there. She had a perfect smile, and I remember thinking, *This is the one*, though of course I didn't know what that meant.

I asked around and got her name—let's call her Rachel Critelli—and found out that she lived right there in Naugatuck. That was great news! We were just kids, and we didn't have cars, so geography was very important to us. If I'd been told she was from Waterbury, I would have had to find another girl to fall in love with.

Unfortunately, I was pathologically shy, so I never approached her. But I thought about her all summer. I'd go to bed at night, thinking of her. And I'd wake up every morning, *still* thinking of her. Then I found out that she'd be attending Naugatuck High that September, and I was in heaven. I knew in my heart that somehow we'd end up together. I was no longer dreading going back to school. I had good reason to go. Hell, I had a reason to *live*.

That first day back, I saw her arriving with one of her little friends. I was upstairs already, in a second-story classroom, and I was looking down at her through the window. I was so excited I could hardly breathe. Yeah, I know, it sounds pathetic. And it *was*. But for the life of me I couldn't bring myself to approach her.

Days went by. The days turned into weeks.

Then, as luck would have it, Rachel became friends with a girl I'll call Rosie, who lived across the street from me. One Friday night Rosie had a bunch of people over, and I went. I wanted to ask Rachel if she'd have a soda with me sometime, and I practiced in my head: "Hey, Rachel. How you doin'? I'm Michael. Michael Bergin. Would you like to go to exciting downtown Naugatuck with me some night? I can guarantee you'll have the time of your life." Boy, I sucked at this, and I knew it. So I asked Rosie if she'd ask Rachel out for me.

"You want me to ask Rachel out?" she said.

"No, you moron. I want you to ask if she'll go out with me."

"Why would she want to go out with you?" Rosie said. "Why would anyone want to go out with you?"

But she was only kidding. She went over and asked, and I waited in the hallway with my heart in my throat. Rosie came back and told me Rachel had said she'd think about it. I didn't know what there was to think about, but apparently Rachel was concerned because she didn't really know me.

"Of course she doesn't know me," I told Rosie. "That's why I'm asking her out. So she'll get to know me."

"Okay," Rosie said. "I'll tell her. I'll get back to you."

Nothing happened. I was waiting for the longest time, torturing myself with worst-case scenarios: *She's laughing at you. She thinks you're a nerd.* I thought maybe I should just be a man about this and go right up to Rachel and start making conversation. But I wasn't all that good at conversation, and even the thought of standing real close to her filled me with fear. I was beginning to break into a sweat—all this deep thought was exhausting—when suddenly a voice called my name. I turned around. It was Rachel. She'd come over like it was the most natural thing in the world, which I guess it was.

"Hi," she said. "I understand you want to ask me out?"

"That's right," I said.

"Okay," she said, then looked at her watch and told me that her mother was coming to get her in about a minute.

"Just when things were getting interesting," I said.

Rachel laughed—I guess I wasn't so bad after all—and suddenly she grabbed me and kissed me right on the mouth. She stopped just as suddenly and ran off without another word, leaving the taste of her on my lips. I was in shock. I stumbled back into the living room and looked through the window, and saw her reaching the street just as her mother pulled up. She turned and looked in my direction, but she must not have seen me. She didn't wave or anything.

Monday, I saw her at school. And neither of us said anything about that hot kiss. But we exchanged numbers, and pretty soon we were hanging out a lot and talking on the phone every day. But we didn't live close enough to get together after school, so our time together was limited.

Finally, on Christmas Eve, her parents had a little party. Rachel asked if I could come. My mom said I could go and drove me out to her house. I met Rachel's family and some of their friends, then she took me up to her room and we made out and fooled around. It was nothing too intense—we were both virgins—but I was in heaven.

I called her several times over the next few days, but I never heard back from her. When I got back to school, I found out she had met this other guy—let's call him Dan Heflin—one of the school studs. Every girl wanted him. I was heartbroken.

I felt like kicking the shit out of Dan Heflin—I'd shot up that year, and I was close to six feet tall—but I've never been one for violence. And tall as I was I still didn't know how to throw a punch. And what the hell was the point anyway? I'd been dumped. So I just acted like I was cool with it. I was nice to her and even friendly with Dan. We'd pass each other in the corridor, and I'd wave and smile, and he'd wave and smile back, like life was wonderful or something, and weren't we just lucky to be growing up in this great little town and going to this great high school. And I realized then what was a big part of life: bullshit.

A year went by. I didn't date anyone. I kept to myself, did my usual brownnosing, and concentrated on my grades. I took driver's ed and got my learner's permit, and every once in a while my father would let me take a spin in the so-called kids' car, a used Aries he had bought for my brother and sister to tool around in. Now that I was old enough to drive, it became my car too.

One day, Rachel saw me pulling into school in the Aries. She came over and asked, "Why don't you take me out on a date?"

"A date?" I said. "What about Dan?"

"He doesn't mind," she said.

"Are you sure?" I said. "If it was me, I'd mind."

"It's not like that with us. He goes out with plenty of other girls."

"Okay," I said. "I'll call you."

That Saturday, I picked her up and drove her to the movies. I felt pretty good behind the wheel. I had my elbow hanging out the window, and I was leaning way back in the seat. It was nice just being there. There was no pressure. We were just hanging out as friends. I felt I could be myself with her, so I relaxed. I had nothing to prove—and nothing to lose either.

We shared a big popcorn during the movie, and laughed at all the same places, and when it was over she suggested we drive over to Hamilton Park, out in Waterbury. We parked and walked out across the grass, under a starry sky. I was so happy that I completely forgot all the pain she'd caused me. Sure, I'd been pretty devastated, but that was then, and this was now, and maybe Rachel realized she'd made a big mistake. I looked up at the moon and thought that life didn't get much better than this. My love for her was strong and pure and true.

She leaned over and kissed me. It was a perfect kiss. Not too short, not too long. But right after the kiss we looked at each other and felt kind of lousy about it. After all, Dan was her boyfriend, and—all things considered—I thought he was a pretty good guy.

"That was wrong, wasn't it?" I said.

She nodded but didn't say anything. We stood up. It was time to go home.

Monday, I got to school and ran into her by the front door. She was standing there with Dan, all cuddly and stuff, laughing at one of his jokes. Dan said hi and I said hi back, and Rachel looked at me and shrugged. I didn't know what I was supposed to read into that shrug; I didn't know whether she was trying to tell me something. I was very confused. I didn't see her around for the rest of the day, so I tried to call her later, at home. I left a message with her mother, but she didn't call me back.

The next day, Dan came up to me in the schoolyard. He didn't look too friendly. "I hear you went out with my girl," he said.

"We just went to a movie."

"That's not what I hear."

"I don't know what you mean," I said, wondering who had ratted us out. Then it hit me that maybe Rachel had told him.

One of Dan's friends showed up. "What are you waiting for?" he told Dan. "If it was me, I'd kick this punk's ass."

I was tall, like I said, but Dan was no shrimp. He didn't do anything. Maybe he was in denial; maybe he couldn't believe that something like this could happen to the school stud. He walked off, with his little buddy whining at him and egging him on. "Man! What's wrong with you? Why didn't you knock Bergin's teeth down his throat?" A lovely image. It stayed with me for a few days.

The following week, early in the morning at school, I was walking down the hallway, minding my own business, when I got tackled from behind and knocked to the ground. It was Dan; he dropped onto my back, knocking the wind out of me, and pinned my arms to my sides, then he grabbed me by the hair and proceeded to bang my head against the ground. I don't know what happened next, but the adrenaline must have been pumping, because suddenly I was on my feet, and he was on his ass. He stood up and came at me again, seriously pissed, and swung twice, missing both times. I wound up and threw a punch of my own—*bam!* I hit him right in the face. It felt good. I did it again. I looked down at my fists. I couldn't believe what I'd just done.

Just then, two teachers came running out of their classrooms and broke it up. They sent us to the principal's office. I didn't give a shit. I felt great. For a little while there, I was thinking that nonviolence was overrated. Sometimes a little violence was good for the soul.

The story got out that Dan was a coward. That he'd tackled me from behind. That I'd popped him twice in the face and that I would have kicked his ass if the teachers hadn't broken it up.

Rachel found me later that day. "I'm sorry about what happened with Dan," she said.

"Me too," I said. "Did you tell him you'd gone to the movies with me?"

"No," she said.

"Who did?"

"I don't know," she said. "But I told him I didn't want to see him anymore."

"You did?"

"Yeah," she said. "I dumped him."

"You dumped him?"

"What are you doing Friday?" she asked.

"I don't know. Why?"

"Why don't you take me out?"

"I don't think that's a good idea."

"Why not?" she said.

I felt like I was being manipulated. I didn't trust her anymore. She'd used me to make him jealous. Maybe everyone thought I was some kind of big hero for popping Dan a couple of times, but the more I thought about it the less I felt like a hero. Sure, I'd felt good about it, for a minute or two. But what had it really done for either of us? I'd never been one for that kind of attention.

Next thing I knew, Rachel was hanging out with my friends, trying to inch her way back into my life. I ignored her, or tried to anyway. It got harder and harder.

"I made a mistake," she told me one day after school. "I'm sorry."

"I'm sorry too," I said, and walked away.

I was still putting in a few hours at the Waterbury Club, mostly on weekends, and I found a second job as a bar-back at this place called

Night Life, down in Waterbury. I wasn't allowed to handle any alcohol, being a minor, so I basically washed glasses, made sure the bartender had plenty of ice on hand, and poured the occasional Coke for a thirsty customer.

One night, this girl with dirty-blond hair came in and took a seat at the bar. She kept eyeballing me. And I eyeballed her right back. I was still a pretty shy kid, but I was kind of trapped there, behind the bar, and we started talking. I'll call her Susan, and she was maybe nineteen or twenty, a couple of years older than I was, and very hot looking. And the more I talked to her, the more excited I got. I had a feeling something was going to happen with this girl.

"What time do you get off?" she asked me.

"Not till about three," I said. This kind of thing didn't happen very often with me. In fact, it *never* happened.

"I'll wait," she said.

We closed up and she hung out while I cleaned up and did what I had to do. We then drove to this park in Prospect, a few miles away. Before I knew it, we were making out pretty heavily, and then we were half naked in back. I was a little nervous—*Am I doing this right? Why is everything so slippery?*—but it was a lot easier than the first time I'd tried this, out in the cold, with one of my friends grinning and egging me on. And while it didn't last long, it was pretty nice. I finally understood what all the fuss was about. On the other hand, I realized I would have enjoyed it a lot more if I'd shared the experience with someone I really cared about.

Susan took care of my awakening sexuality for a few weeks, then she took some out-of-state job and left town. I never saw her again. I realized I never really knew all that much about her. When we got together, it was purely about sex. I'm not sure she ever told me her last name. We were there to get laid.

Suddenly I missed getting laid. One night in early 1986 I was out at the local 7-Eleven with two of my friends, eating nachos and cheese, thinking about getting laid, and talking about getting laid, and wondering where young studs like us might go to get laid, when a couple of potheads pulled up in a pickup truck and started racing around the parking lot. On one of the turns, they got a little too close for comfort, and words were exchanged. The next thing I knew we were mixing it up, the cops were called, and we all got dragged away in cuffs.

It was pretty awful. Me, the son of a cop, getting arrested for disturbing the peace. My old man came down to the precinct to get me. And to see him there, looking down at me, looking embarrassed to have a kid like me, was terrible. It would have been easier to do hard time.

I told him I was sorry, that it would never happen again. And he just said over and over how disappointed he was.

"I never expected this from you, Michael," he said. "You are just looking for trouble."

He was pretty cold to me for a few days, and I saw how a father's disappointment can be a very powerful tool.

At school, I again began to find myself hanging around with Rachel. We were sort of in the same clique, and I was seeing her almost every day. I was really drawn to her, and I was suddenly kicking myself for having told her that I didn't want to get back together.

One afternoon that spring, I was playing racquetball down at the YMCA, and Rachel showed up. We ended up playing together, and I drove her home. We parked down the street from her house and made out for about four hours. It was pretty good. My lips were chapped and sore. We were back. Well, sort of. We kept breaking up with each other, usually without any reason, and we kept getting back together, without any reason for that either. We had one of those on-again, off-again relationships, and it lasted for the better part of the next decade.

Love. Go figure.

By my senior year in high school, I was playing varsity basketball and I'd made the all-state baseball team. Still, as good as I was, I realized it wasn't going to pay the bills.

My parents wanted me to go to college of course. As my father put it, over and over again, "Get an education. It's the one thing no one can ever take away from you."

So I focused on my studies, kept up my grades, and applied to college. I took Rachel to prom, we stayed out late, and I crashed at her place. In the morning a whole group of us went to the beach at Hammonasset State Park, right there in Connecticut, where we drank, played volleyball, swam, and marveled at the fact that we were done with high school. Now we had to worry about college and the rest of our lives, which was a pretty tall order.

I figured I might go into law enforcement, like my old man, but I was thinking about doing it on a federal level: I began to imagine myself as an FBI agent. I considered New Haven University because it had a very solid criminology department, and I applied to both the University of Connecticut and Northeastern University in Boston. None of these places were free, so I immediately buckled down and went to work for a mason. In the weeks and months ahead, I learned more about putting up walls than I wanted to know. I built chimneys and laid foundations. I mixed concrete, carried cinder blocks, and struggled under the groaning weight of overloaded wheelbarrows. It was grueling work, but it had an upside: by the end of July, I was in the best shape of my life.

I lived at home all summer and saved every penny I made. My father already had two kids in college, and I didn't want to further strain the family finances. When it came time to make a decision on where I was going to end up, I opted for the University of Connecticut, Home of the Huskies. It was a state school and much less expensive than Northeastern. But even with all that backbreaking work I only had enough money for the first semester. My old man could see that I was serious about my education, so he volunteered to pay for the second semester. I told him I hoped that one day I could pay him back, although I suspected he would never allow it.

I can't say I got off to a great start in college. There was never any shortage of parties. And the girls were pretty friendly too.

I took up briefly with a girl I'll call Nancy. She was from Town Plot, a very tight-knit community at the edge of Waterbury, where the guys happened to be a little territorial about their women. One night, Nancy and I went to the Safari Club, out in Waterbury, with my friend Tommy and this other girl, who also happened to be from Town Plot. And sure enough, a couple of these Town Plot guys started messin' with us about being with *their* women, and the messin' turned into nasty taunts, and the taunts turned into an all-out brawl. The next thing I knew, I was being led away in cuffs, and shouting at the arresting officer: "How dare you call yourself a cop?! My father's a *real* cop, pal, and he'll have your badge!"

My father came down to the station, again; he bailed me out, again. He was pretty steamed. "Never gonna happen again, huh?" he said, throwing my words in my face.

I tried to explain how it went down: "We were just mindin' our own business. And these guys, like, just started harassin' us," but it sounded pretty lame. So I gave up and we drove home in silence. I apologized again when we got there and once more as we stepped into the house, but my father didn't say anything. He wanted to let his disappointment register.

I was pretty bummed. I decided I had to buckle down and start taking my studies seriously. And that's exactly what I did. I studied and ate pizza and studied some more. And when I wasn't studying or eating pizza, I was waiting tables at Phil's Steak & Lobster House in Waterbury. They fed me there too—though not on steak or lobster. I got mostly garlic bread and pasta. And one day I looked down at myself and saw that I was putting on a little weight. I had a regular gut on me—that old beer-and-pizza gut. And I didn't like it. Part of it was sheer vanity of course, but part of it was the way I'd felt the previous summer, working that masonry gig, when I'd been in the best shape of my life.

I started running and hitting the gym and lifting and doing crunches. And by April I was back in shape. I also happened to be damn near broke. The tips at Phil's were good and everything, but I needed real money for my sophomore year tuition, and I hadn't saved a penny.

Then I heard from a friend about this builder who was looking for help. I'll call him Vito. I went out to see him and liked him right away. He was a great guy, warm, friendly, with a beautiful wife and two beautiful kids. And he was incredibly successful. I mean, by Naugatuck standards, he lived in a mansion. But he didn't throw it in my face or anything. He made himself seem like a regular schmo, just like me.

I worked with him all summer. Commercial construction, mostly. And you've got to picture it: the middle of a heat wave and we'd be hauling lumber, bricks, and pipes around all day. It wasn't easy work, but I kept going because I was making ten bucks an hour, and the numbers were adding up.

In September, when I went back to school, Vito asked me to keep working for him. He said I should just put in hours whenever I could, and to please keep track of my time. So I was out there most weekends, throughout fall and into winter, when I was suddenly freezing and found myself longing for summer. And of course I was out there in the spring, when the snow melted and everyone discovered all sorts of wonderful new leaks in their roofs and decks. Vito would track me down in the dorm in the middle of the night with some emergency or other and ask if I could please come out at the crack of dawn and give him a hand.

I worked for him all spring and through a second summer, and I was barely managing to keep ahead of my bills. But as August drew to a close, a terrible thing happened: I couldn't find Vito anywhere. I'd call or go by the house or wait for him at the office, but he was never there. The guy still owed me $2,500, and I needed the money for school.

When I finally caught up with him, he gave me a couple hundred bucks, cash, and told me he'd have the rest of it by Friday. But Friday rolled around, and Vito was nowhere to be found.

I had heard that he'd been screwing around with drugs, and I thought it was maybe pot or something small. But now I was hearing that it was much more serious, that Vito had a little heroin problem. And then I found out that the problem wasn't so damn little.

He was booking jobs left and right, but he wasn't interested in doing the work. He was taking the money—a one-third deposit, up front—and putting it in his veins. And he was pulling it off too. For a while anyway. Old Vito, with that big warm smile of his, telling the potential customer that he'd give him a good deal. "I'm going to do this for you as a personal favor, because I knew your father, God rest his soul." Good old Vito. That warmth coming through. And so *convincing*. I saw it with my own eyes one time when I tracked him down to ask again about my money. He was sweet-talking this little old couple. "Crew'll be here Monday," he said, smiling his trademark good-guy smile. "Crack of dawn. We'll have the job done in three days."

And of course there was no crew. It was only me and a couple of other guys who were still hanging in. I was hanging in because I was desperate. I didn't know why those other guys were still there.

"I need my money, Vito," I said over and over again.

"And you're gonna get it too," Vito replied. He'd put his big arm around my shoulders and lead me back to the car. "I'm a little strapped this week, but I should have it for you next week. Why you lookin' at me like that? You think I'd screw you? I wouldn't screw a kid like you. College kid and everything! Trying to make a life for yourself. Trying to build a real future."

I guess you know the answer to that question. Yeah, he screwed me. And everyone else, especially that nice family of his. I tried to get my money one more time, toward the end of the summer, but by then the son of a bitch was gone. He told everyone I was a cheat and a liar; he said he couldn't believe I would make up those outrageous stories about him owing me money and such—*him,* who was only trying to help, who only had my best interests at heart, who had treated me like family.

Before long, it was clear to everyone that *he* was the bad guy, not me. Too many people came out of the woodwork with complaints. Lawsuits were filed.

Only his wife and kids stood by him. She should have known better, but she was in denial. She could see their life crumbling. Their bills were unpaid. Creditors were knocking on the door. Collection agencies were calling.

And when she was told about the drugs, when evidence of heroin use was literally thrown in her face, she still refused to believe any of it.

Months later, he disappeared, leaving her and the kids to fend for themselves. He turned up in Florida weeks later, calling from jail, begging for help. But it was too late. He was tens of thousands of dollars in debt, and no one had that kind of money. And even if they did, why help the son of a bitch now? After everything he'd done.

Such a waste of a life. And such destruction in his wake. I wasn't even twenty at the time, but it taught me something about drugs. They can take a good man, a warm, funny, loving family man, and turn him into a loser and worse. He was a good guy, Vito. That smile, the gift of gab. He was the go-to builder for miles around, and for years no one heard anything but good stories about him and the fine work he did. But drugs ended it. Drugs turned Vito into a criminal. No one ever heard from him again. No one knew what happened to him. And at that point no one cared.

That experience taught me to watch myself around drugs. It also taught me to be cautious in business. I heard this great line once: "Always approach a business deal as if the other person is trying to screw you. He probably is. And, if he isn't, you'll be pleasantly surprised."

It's worth remembering. It has always worked for me. Well, mostly.

So my finances were pretty tight, and even though I was putting in a lot more hours at Phil's Steak & Lobster, I was still coming up short. I was desperate. I started mowing lawns, washing windows, painting houses. Then I heard about the resident assistant program. There were students in every dorm who were in charge of enforcing rules and reporting problems. There wasn't much money involved, but in exchange for a little easy work the college waived your room and board. It was an awesome deal.

I figured it was too late to apply, but there had been a problem at my dorm a few weeks earlier—some of the kids got a little rowdy and began tossing toilets through the windows—and the RA in charge had immediately lost his job. So, yeah, there was an opening. I made a good case for myself. And since my grades were good and I'd pretty much kept out of trouble since the melee at the Safari Club, I got the job.

There was nothing to it. I was basically there to keep the peace. If some kids were making too much noise, I'd go over and ask them to please keep it down. If there was drinking in the lobby, I told the kids to take it back to their rooms. And if the smell of marijuana began wafting into the hallways, I'd suggest a visit to the great outdoors. I was about the easiest-going RA these kids had ever had, and they returned the favor by toeing the line.

So I did my RA thing, studied hard, and put in my hours at Phil's. I was working Fridays and Saturdays now, and making pretty good tips. I was also having a fling with one of the waitresses. She was thirty-three and divorced and wasn't looking for much, so after work we'd find some place to park, get it on, and then I'd hustle back to the dorm to make sure no one had set fire to the place.

Then I got another gig as an escort. No, not that kind of escort. I worked with the campus security police, escorting girls to and from their dorms late at night. There was a whole team of us out there, roaming the grounds, seven nights a week. We were equipped with walkie-talkies. A call would come in—some coed is leaving the library, needs an escort—and whoever was closest hustled over and did the job. I think some of the guys were in it to meet girls, but I didn't meet any girls. I had my divorcée, anyway, and she kept me happy.

One Saturday in November of my sophomore year, at Phil's, I tripped with a full tray and managed to drive a wedge of broken glass deep into my knee. I limped home, went to bed, and awoke to find a flyer under my door. It was from some kind of campus men's group. Gay guys. It looked like they were out recruiting.

I wasn't interested in joining their ranks of course, but I was curious about their lifestyle. I was pretty naive in those days, and I couldn't for the life of me understand what a man could possibly see in another man. As to what they actually *did* together, well, that was completely beyond me. But at that moment I realized that I hadn't fulfilled one of my key responsibilities as the dorm's RA. When I was offered the job, I'd been told that I was expected to make some kind of "educational contribution" to the students under my care, and the flyer in my hand seemed to be a perfect opportunity.

So I called the number and spoke to the guy in charge—a very sweet guy, as I recall—and a week later he and several of his friends were sitting in the lobby of the dorm, talking to my group about homosexuality. I found it quite illuminating. I had grown up with typical small-town prejudices. In my neighborhood, one of the worst things you could do to a guy was call him a faggot. And I called plenty of guys faggots, long before I even knew what a faggot was. But there I was, listening to these guys. They were well spoken, and they enunciated very clearly, and they were nicely groomed too. Initially, there were a few snickers from my group, but I started jotting down names, which ended that pretty quickly. Suddenly everyone was listening politely, discovering that gay people are just like regular people—just looking for love and companionship too—and when the talk was over they went home. And that was that. But, as I said, I did find the talk illuminating. Some of these guys had struggled with homosexuality all their lives, and they were very candid about it. To be honest with you, I found that kind of honesty and openness very refreshing. I came from a community where a man kept his feelings to himself. Now I was learning that just because a man is different, and just because he is honest about his differences, didn't make him any less of a person.

The following weekend, I was back in Naugatuck, visiting my family, and one night I ran into someone I'll refer to as Judy Bunker, an old friend of my parents, at a bar. Her husband, who I'll call Roy, was a carpenter who had built the deck in our backyard. Mrs. Bunker recognized me right away. She came over and said a big hello and told me that she couldn't believe how much I'd changed over the years.

"I can't believe how good-looking you've gotten!" she said over and over.

"Yeah, right!" I said.

"No," she said. "I'm serious. You're a gorgeous young man. Have you ever considered modeling?"

"No," I said. And I hadn't. What's more, I didn't think I was particularly good-looking. I certainly didn't think I looked anything like the men in magazines.

"Well you should think about it," she said. "You have the look for it, and you seem to have the body for it. Those boys make lots of money. As much as a thousand dollars a day!"

"Get out!" I said. "A thousand dollars a day?! To stand in front of a camera?!" That was fortune. It couldn't be real. I said good-bye to Mrs. Bunker and thanked her for saying all those wonderful things about me, then went back to the bar to hang with my friends, but I didn't give it another thought that night.

Still, when I got back to college, I couldn't get the notion out of my head. I stared at my reflection in the mirror. It was true: I wasn't bad looking. And I was in pretty good physical shape. And how could it hurt? I was making a few bucks waiting tables at Phil's, sure, but it was nowhere near enough. And by that time I'd given up on ever seeing the money Vito owed me.

So I dug up a tattered copy of the yellow pages and called several local modeling agencies. None of them would see me of course, but they all asked me to send pictures. I had a friend take a roll of snapshots, half of them shirtless, and submitted them to several of the agencies. I didn't hear anything for several weeks, then the responses started trickling in. They all said they had a guy who looked just like me, amazingly enough, which was the standard pass, I guess.

Then I heard from an agency in Stanford. The rep left a message that I should set up a meeting, so I called to make arrangements and drove over the following week. He was very nice. He said he loved me, loved my look, and that I was going to need to put together a zed card. He explained that this was the industry standard, a calling card that contained a head shot, a body shot, and on the flip side a résumé. As luck would have it, this guy was not only a modeling rep but also a photographer. And since I was new to the business, he would cut his regular price to a mere three hundred dollars. I guess I hadn't learned my lesson about the murky world of business, because I immediately accepted his offer.

And wouldn't you know it, he actually had time to shoot me that very afternoon. He ushered me into the room next door and we got started.

"Look sexy."

"Look pouty."

"Look serious."

"Look hot."

It was a little embarrassing, to be honest. I felt like a narcissistic fool. I couldn't get comfortable. I had hoped to feel like John Travolta must have felt in *Saturday Night Fever*—you know, punching his fist into the air and striking a pose—but I just felt painfully uncomfortable.

A week later, a package of two hundred zed cards arrived in the mail for me at college. The shots looked okay, but they didn't seem all that professional—even to my untrained eye. The résumé was pretty lame: Michael Bergin is pursuing a business degree at the University of Connecticut. He has worked as a waiter and a roofer, and is currently a resident assistant in his dorm. Boy, wouldn't that just make you want to run out and hire me?!

I didn't know what the hell I was supposed to do with the zed cards, and I kept calling my agent/photographer and missing him. I began to wonder whether I'd ever hear from him again. Then early one evening he called back.

"Michael," he said. "I have good news. I got you a job!"

The job was the following Sunday, out in Greenwich. I showed up at a popular neighborhood grocery store, looking as Hawaiian as possible, in a flowery print shirt, three-quarter pants, sandals, and a makeshift lei, and I stood out front giving away these second-rate potato chips from Maui. (That's where they were supposed to be from anyway. I think they were actually made in New Jersey.) I felt like a real dork.

"Hey, would you like some free chips?"

"You gotta try these Maui chips. They make you feel like you're on the Islands."

"I guarantee that these are the best chips you've ever had. And I guarantee it personally." Nod nod, wink wink.

My biggest fear was that I'd run into someone I knew, but Greenwich was pretty far from my regular stomping grounds, so I stopped worrying and focused on the hard and intellectually challenging day ahead of me. I spent eight hours grinning at complete strangers, foisting greasy chips on them, and making small talk about fat content and such. It was my first modeling gig, and already I was filled with doubt. On the other hand, I was getting seventy-five bucks for an eight-hour day, which seemed pretty good to me.

When I got back to school, I called my agent and left a message asking how I did. I know, I know, it sounds a little silly, but it was my first job. I wanted him to be impressed. He didn't return my calls.

"Hey," I said when I finally reached him, almost a week later. "It's me, Michael. Michael Bergin." I was trying not to sound too hurt. "I've been trying to reach you for a week."

"I've been busy," he said. He made it sound like he had a stable of hugely successful clients, and that I'd never be one of them.

"Well, yeah, sorry," I said. "I was calling to see how it went."

"You were great," he said. "A regular Laurence Olivier."

All right. Enough of this shit. "What about my seventy-five dollars?" I said.

"Seventy-five dollars?" he shot back. "What about my time? What about the cost of mailing out the zed cards?"

I was too tired to protest. I hung up and went back to my lonely room and tried to scrape together enough change for a sandwich. I'm not kidding. I was pretty broke. And there was no food service at the college on weekends. I remember finding just enough money for a six-inch sandwich at the local Subway. I could have eaten two of the foot-longs, but all I could afford was one bite-sized sandwich—*without* a soda. My hat's off to anyone who has ever struggled. I struggled. Then again, I must confess that I'm luckier than most people. My parents weren't all that far away. Every second weekend, I'd go home and eat like a pig—and that was before dinner.

One early Sunday morning in May, I was sitting on the family couch, recuperating after a gargantuan breakfast, when my father walked in, lugging his golf clubs. He had just played eighteen holes with his old friend who I'll call Joe Maresca, and he had told Mr. Maresca about me and this modeling thing. It turned out that Mr. Maresca had a son who used to be a model in New York City. The son lived right there in Naugatuck, in fact, and my father just happened to have gotten his number.

So I called Joe Jr. and he said he'd be happy to talk to me. I went over that same day. He was close to thirty, married, with two kids. And he'd been out of the business for a while. But he retrieved the old portfolio and went through it, and I could see how much he enjoyed reminiscing about the old days.

I told him about my experience with the Stanford agent.

"Those guys are all bullshit," he said.

"So I discovered."

"If you don't mind dressing up as a hot dog and barking at complete strangers, stay in Connecticut. But if you want to get serious about modeling, New York's the answer."

Then I made the mistake of asking him why he got out, and he said it wasn't really his choice. "I made a few bucks here and there," he said. "But I knew I was never going to turn it into a career. That was pretty obvious, pretty fast. So it's not like I got out exactly. Plus, I had a family to support."

"Sounds rough," I said.

"It is," he said. "It's very competitive. But if you hit, you can hit big."

He gave me a list of some respectable agencies, and I thanked him for his time and went on my way.

Here's the thing: I was twenty years old and lived less than two hours from New York City and—hard as it is to believe—I'd never been there. Not once. Worse, I'd never even been all that curious about going. It was just a big city, right?

I dug up a Manhattan phone book, looked up the agencies on Joe Jr.'s list, and put together a plan of attack. Finally, the big day arrived. I got into my acid-washed jeans and my wife-beater T-shirt, grabbed two dozen of my zed cards, and hooked up with my father for the ride to the train station.

"Don't believe everything you hear," he said as we drove over. "And be careful. New York is a big place."

Wow. Grand Central Station. *Big* didn't begin to describe it, and I hadn't even left the station. When I finally stepped out into the city, I felt like a wide-eyed kid. I'd seen New York in countless movies and television shows, but nothing had prepared me for the real thing. The size of the buildings. The noise. Streets teeming with people. And everyone moving moving moving.

I stopped at the nearest newsstand, got a map of the subway system, and began to plot out my day. I did fairly well from an organizational point of view—I was able to find every agency on my list—but I didn't do as well in every other respect. I didn't realize that I couldn't just walk in off the street, that these were very busy people. I was expected to call ahead and make an appointment.

Toward the end of the day, with only three more agencies on my list, I lucked out. Another thing I hadn't realized was that some of the agencies actually had open calls once a week, and I arrived at Elite to find some thirty or forty good-looking people milling around the lobby.

"What's going on?" I asked someone.

"We're waiting," he said.

Just then, a set of doors swung open and out came a big woman with big glasses. Everyone fell silent. She paced back and forth, checking us out. No one said anything. It was as if they were afraid to breathe. Consequently, I was afraid to breathe too. Then the woman started talking, and it struck me that her repertoire was limited to two words: "stay" and "go." The latter seemed to be more popular.

When it was over, there were only five of us left. I was one of them. I was also the first one she invited into the inner sanctum.

I sat across a small desk from her and showed her my zed card. "A resident assistant. Oh my!" She didn't seem all that impressed.

"Well," she said finally, peering at me through her big glasses, "you're the right height, and I like your look, but we already have several boys with the same look. And you have no training or experience."

I was beginning to wonder what I was doing there. Was this some kind of test? How well will Michael Bergin stand up to insult and torture?

"I could get experience," I ventured, knowing I sounded lame. But she must not have thought so.

"Yes," she said. "You could. And you *must*. I'm going to give you the names of a few smaller agencies that might be interested in you. Go out and make waves, and come back to see us when you're ready."

I left feeling pretty grim. She'd been nice and all, but I didn't know whether I had it in me. I had walked into a roomful of good-looking people, most of them better looking than me, and only a handful had made it into her office. I was one of them, but the payoff had been less than inspiring: Go forth and get experience.

I made my way back toward Grand Central, convinced with each step that this business really wasn't for me, and that I'd been a fool to think otherwise, when I realized that one of the agencies she had suggested was on that very block. I was staring right at the sign. The Big Guy in the Sky must have been trying to tell me something.

I leaned on the buzzer. Someone let me in. I told the young lady at the reception desk that I'd just come from Elite, and I guess it was the right thing to say. A moment later, I was in back with one of the bookers. He loved me. He loved my zed card. He started putting the agency sticker on it.

"You're going to need a new card," he said. "A whole new card. Something, um, a little more professional. New head shots. New body shots. I can't possibly send this out."

Then why was he putting his sticker on it? What was he so excited about?

"I'm going to give you a list of photographers," he went on. It was obvious that people in New York City were big on lists. "You'll make an appointment and ask him to shoot two or three rolls. It shouldn't cost you more than forty or fifty dollars. Get a quote up front."

It felt like more of the same, only different. At least this guy sounded legitimate. Had he tried to usher me into the back room for a shoot, I would have known better. Still, did I really want to do this? I thought about it all the way back to Connecticut. By the time the train pulled into the station, I had decided to give it one last shot. I kept thinking about Mrs. Bunker: "Those boys make lots of money. As much as a thousand dollars a day!" And what did I have to lose but my pride?

The next day, I got through to David Bird, one of the photographers who had been recommended by Mr. Enthusiasm. I made an appointment to come into the city the following week. He told me to bring several outfits—jeans, shirts, T-shirts, dress slacks, a sports coat or two, et cetera—and I borrowed what I didn't have and got back on the train.

David Bird was very courteous and professional. He made me feel as if I were entering a whole new world, a world far removed from Naugatuck. He was incredibly patient. He explained every shot: the way the lights worked, the mood he was after, what he needed from me and why.

I smiled and pouted and flexed and looked angry and changed in and out of my paltry outfits, worrying about my performance. Before I knew it, the shoot was over. But apparently David Bird wasn't done with me. He picked up the phone and called a friend at a local agency. "Listen," he said. "I've got this guy here, Michael Bergin. You should take a look at him."

As it turned out, he was talking to someone at Click, which was one of the top male agencies in New York, and apparently the rep took David Bird's recommendations very seriously. The next thing I knew I was back in my acid-washed jeans, on my way to Click.

Click liked me too and signed me on the spot. I was told to start building a respectable portfolio, which was done by going out to "test" with various photographers. There wasn't any money in it of course, but they urged me not to worry about money—not for the moment anyway. For the moment the only thing that mattered was building the portfolio, and that's what the photographers were for. A model was nothing without a portfolio. *Less* than nothing. "Let's change that as quickly as we can!" they said.

I also needed to get a haircut. My hair was short, but the booker wanted it even shorter. And I was told to stop lifting weights. The abs were perfect, but the rest of me was too big. They thought I wouldn't fit into the clothes. So I went home and had my mother give me a haircut—I looked like a porcupine for a few days—and I gave up weight training for cardio. It was amazing. Within a week, I'd become a smaller, leaner version of my old self.

Now I began to commute into the city regularly. I'd book time with a photographer, hop on the train, make my way over to his studio, and let him do his thing. It always felt a little cold though. Most of the photographers were quite young, just breaking into the business themselves. They were busy putting together their portfolios as photographers, and I was busy putting together my portfolio as a model. We were all pretty much in the same boat: young guys trying to break into the biz. We were all a little desperate and self-absorbed and focused on making it. As a result, there was never much time for pleasant conversation—or conversation of any kind, come to think of it. I'd go in, do what I was told, put my shirt back on, and go home.

I do, however, remember one exception. I'll call him Mitch Fraser. Professionally speaking, he was leaps and bounds ahead of all the other photographers I had tested with. Strangely enough, he was also the most personable. He took his time with me. Talked to me. Told me repeatedly that I had the makings of stardom. When he found out I'd come in on the train, all the way from Connecticut, he told me that I could crash at his place any time I wanted. And when I left, he gave me his home number. "If you ever need anything, call me," he said. "Or call me if you *don't* need anything. I'm around. And my offer stands."

As the weeks turned into months, I started learning a little something about this business of fashion. I had heard the big names: Giorgio Armani. Calvin Klein. Ralph Lauren. But they had never meant much to me beyond my boxers. I didn't know the first thing about clothes. I got my jeans at Bob's Surplus Store. Seriously.

Through all of this, I somehow managed to get through my junior year at UConn. Summer came and went and I was still getting my jeans at Bob's Surplus. I had worked very hard, but I hadn't made a penny. Still, I wasn't complaining. This was the nature of the beast. And I really felt that I was on the right track.

So I did the unthinkable. I decided to skip the first semester of my senior year. I called the school and explained that I had to take a semester off for personal reasons, and I made those reasons sound sufficiently grim. Officials at the school were very understanding. They not only refunded my tuition—all the money I'd made waiting tables at Phil's, mowing lawns, painting houses—but assured me that I could come back at any time, and that they'd even see about making me an RA again.

Then I did a difficult thing for a twenty-year-old: I moved back in with my parents. And I waited by the phone. The phone would ring, and it would be one of the bookers at Click, but every time it was the same thing: "Are you available at two today?" "Can you be at Bloomingdale's in an hour?"

I was still in the very early phase of what I hoped would become a lucrative career, and the only opportunities that presented themselves tended to do so on very short notice. So I was always rushing. And usually not making it. And when I got a little advance notice, it was almost worse. I had to take the train from Naugatuck to Bridgeport, and from Bridgeport to Grand Central. I'd often leave the house in the wee hours, when it was still dark and cold, and I generally didn't make it home until after ten. It made for long, exhausting days. Plus, it was costing me a small fortune. There was the train fare, for starters, and there was travel within the city. I also had to feed myself. I tried to keep it cheap, but even a slice of pizza feels expensive when you've got no money coming in.

I'd return home, exhausted, and sit around the following day recovering and waiting by the phone. The family found it a little odd, but mostly they kept their thoughts to themselves. Not my brother though. He really enjoyed ribbing me, especially about my hair. I'd just discovered hair gel, and he couldn't find enough to say about it.

"So how's the Gel Master this morning? Catch any flies in there?"

I took the ribbing. It wasn't that bad. And when it got bad, I'd go over to see Rachel Critelli. She was as beautiful as ever. I forgave her all her trespasses against me, and we hooked up again. She was studying fashion design. She was the only person in Naugatuck who seemed to think I'd make it in the big bad world of fashion, and, to this day, I still appreciate her faith and kind words. Even though she did dump me. Again. And again. And again.

Then, at long last, a miracle: my very first paying job. I was asked to model clothes for *Gentlemen's Quarterly*, or *GQ*, as the magazine is commonly known. My day started with an early morning train ride to Manhattan. At ten o'clock, I showed up at the *GQ* offices and slipped into a three-piece suit, posed for Polaroids, then was sent off to change and start all over again. These were called "fittings." The point was to show the clothes to the editorial staff at the magazine, so they could pick the outfits they liked best, and then shoot them on *real* models. In short, I was a human coat hanger.

The shoot went on for nine hours a day for three days and paid a whopping fifty dollars. The agency took twenty percent of that, of course, and the government wasn't shy about taxes. So I was making about two dollars and fifty cents an hour. At the end of three days, given my expenses, I had actually lost money. But it was *GQ*; it was a start.

My next gig, several weeks later, was with Diesel. There I got paid fifty bucks an hour for the same job, so clearly I was moving up in the world. But there was a catch: sometimes I was only needed for an hour. I'd get up at the crack of dawn, make my way into the city, pose for a few shots, and go home. I did the math. If I included travel time, I was still making about two-fifty an hour. So maybe I wasn't moving up after all. Then again, there were days when they needed me for two hours. And, on rare occasions, *three* or *four*. At that stage, we were talking serious profits.

One day, Diesel asked me to shoot a video for them. I got a thousand dollars for one day's work. I was in heaven. When I got to see the video, I thought I looked like a movie star.

This went to my head—but in a good way. I decided I was going to make a career out of modeling, and the only way I could possibly do so was by moving to New York City. But I also wanted to finish college. So I put the move off for a year. It was sheer hell, a real balancing act. Studying, commuting, posing, pouting. For a time there, I was convinced that I would fail as both student and model.

The worst of it was when Click called at the last minute with Something Big. An Armani campaign, say. I wanted it—God, how I wanted it!—but unless they sent a chopper for me I'd never make it. And they didn't send a chopper.

One morning, back in Connecticut, I got a call from Click with good news. Bruce Weber wanted me to test with him, and even *I* knew that he was one of the hottest photographers in the business. I was asked to show up at his loft, downtown on Watt Street, on a Friday night at seven. I thought this was pretty strange, but then it got even stranger.

"He's going to ask you to take your clothes off," the booker said. "We have a good relationship with Bruce, and we trust him of course, and the pictures aren't going to go anywhere. But it's really up to you. Clothes or no clothes, it's your call."

I showed up Friday night at seven, as instructed. Bruce himself answered the door. He's short and stocky, and was wearing one of his trademark bandannas.

"Come in, come in," he said in a gentle voice, bowing and backing away from the door. He seemed reluctant to shake my hand. "Thank you for accommodating me. I know it's a little unusual to come to a shoot at this hour."

The loft was large and cluttered. There was stuff everywhere. Photographs. Camera equipment. Assorted junk. Huge filing cabinets occupied one entire wall, and there was a table in the corner with a lit backdrop on the wall, for viewing negatives. A thin wire was strung in the corner between two walls, with several photographs hanging from it, all of them badly warped.

"This way, this way," Bruce said. He bowed and led me off to the far corner of the room. There was a tiled area there that looked like it had once been part of a large shower, but there was no shower. "Why don't you make yourself comfortable," he said. "We can start just as you are, in your T-shirt and jeans."

I didn't know exactly what to do. Bruce reached for one of several cameras and started shooting. I smiled. I clowned a little. I had been nervous coming through the door—Bruce Weber was the Steven Spielberg of the fashion world—but he was making me feel right at ease. Of course we were alone in the place, which was a little off-putting. Most photographers had assistants. Even the neo-phytes. That had been my experience anyway.

"Why don't you take your shirt off, Michael?"

I took my shirt off. "Nice, very nice." He kept shooting.

"Why don't you take your pants off?"

I took my pants off.

"That's it, yes. Press up against the wall there. Yes, flex those muscles. Very nice indeed. Oh yes."

I guess it was good for him. And frankly I didn't mind. I had worked very hard to get my body into this shape, and if showing a little skin was going to get me work—so be it.

"Why don't you drop the briefs?" he said.

Jesus. What was it the agency had told me? That it was my call?

I dropped the briefs.

"Turn this way. Good. Very nice. Very very nice."

He looked as if he was working up a sweat, and maybe he was, because suddenly it was over. "Thank you," he said. "Thank you very much. Thank you for coming." He bowed again, asked me to get dressed, then walked me to the door.

I thought that was pretty strange. The whole thing had taken maybe ten minutes. As I made my way back to Grand Central, I tried to figure out what had just happened. There were only two possibilities. Either Bruce Weber didn't like me, or he didn't like my look. I was confused.

Next morning, bright and early, back in Connecticut, the phone rang. It was the agency again. "Bruce really really liked you," the booker said. "Can you go back tonight, same time?"

"Tonight? Same time?"

"I think it's worth it, Michael. He's testing a lot of younger models for an upcoming Versace campaign. This could be good for you. This could be it."

"Fine," I said. "I'm there."

I went. Same place, same time, same routine. Only this time I got naked faster. I was feeling pretty good. This was Bruce Weber. A master. And he *really really* liked me. He kept firing away, pumping off so many shots that I began to wonder whether there was any film in the camera.

"You seem a little tense, Michael."

"I do?" I said. "I don't feel tense. I feel pretty good, actually."

"No," he insisted. "You seem tense. Come here. Let me help you. I know a wonderful Chinese relaxation technique."

Great! That was all I needed.

He set a blanket on the hardwood floor and had me lie down on it, faceup. Then he crouched by my head and started massaging my temples. He rubbed his hands through my hair. I closed my eyes and tried to relax. He worked my jaw, my shoulders, my neck. Suddenly I was finding it a tad harder to relax. Now he was at my chest. I began to detect a pattern here. Hmmm. Starts at the top, works his way down. Where is he headed, I wonder?

Please keep in mind that I was butt-naked on the floor of this man's loft, with no other human beings in sight—no one to come running if I squealed for help.

"Bruce," I said, and I sat bolt upright. "If you're trying to make me relax, it's not working."

"Really?" he said. "I find that very surprising. This *always* works."

I was sure it did. With lots of guys. But date number two wasn't going all that well for us.

And that was it. The shoot was over. I grabbed my clothes and booked the hell out of there.

The Versace campaign went forward as planned. I wasn't part of it.

A month later, the phone rang. It was the agency again. Bruce had called. He was shooting a Calvin Klein underwear campaign. He had picked ten male models from around the world, the ten best-looking bodies he could find, and only two of them were from the States. "Guess who's on the list?" the booker asked me.

"Me?"

"Right," she said.

I went. Bruce was very nice. If I had hurt his feelings, he didn't let it show. I spent two days prancing around a studio in Queens in my underwear with nine other guys. Bruce must have been in heaven.

They were long days. And when I took travel time into account, I figured I was averaging about six dollars an hour. But what the hell—it was Calvin Klein. The final ad consisted of one shot, and only two out of the ten models were in it. I wasn't one of them, and I was seriously bummed.

But the agency didn't give up on me. "It happens," they said. "More often than you can imagine." They kept sending me out. And they tried to help me in other ways. I remember one of the bookers taking me aside one day and asking, very sweetly, if she could tell me "something personal."

"Sure," I said.

"Those acid-washed jeans have got to go."

I thought acid-washed jeans were cool. And they were—in Naugatuck. In Manhattan, the acid-washed look wasn't happening. She suggested I get a pair of Levi's, and I did. And I felt less like a rube. Marginally.

I guess the agency was used to us small-town guys. We were expected to be a little slow, socially speaking, and I know I didn't disappoint. When I was introduced to Gianni, I thought they'd said Johnny. What did I know from Versace?

But these social gaffes didn't stand in my way. I was getting more work and actually making a few bucks.

That winter, in 1990, I got a call about a movie gig. Me, Michael Bergin—I was going to be a star. The film was called *Whispers in the Dark*, and it starred Alan Alda, Deborah Ungar, and Annabella Sciorra. At the audition, the casting director made me take off my clothes—every last stitch—despite the fact that the role required no frontal nudity. I'd been there, done that. So I didn't mind. He took several Polaroids of me. I figured he was going to show them to his friends. I didn't mind that either. It's showbiz, right?

Amazingly, I got the job, and the shoot took place two weeks later. I was part of a dream sequence. I sat on this upraised platform, naked, facing a beautiful girl, equally naked. I was asked to rub my hands over her breasts. I did. She liked it.

Then the director really began to tax my acting skills. I was asked to simulate oral sex. I was asked to pretend I was taking her from behind. I was asked to assume the missionary position.

It was very embarrassing. I had to keep excusing myself because thinking about just baseball and peanuts wasn't keeping me from getting an erection. I was actually so horny that I was in pain. And so was she. On the last hour of the last day, it actually got a little cold in there, and they covered us with a sheet. The director liked the way it looked, so he began to shoot it with the sheet, and he asked us for a little more *simulation*.

I was on top of her, simulating away, and I was excited. And finally she couldn't take it anymore. She clenched her teeth and whispered in my ear, "Goddamn it, Michael. Don't do this to me! Put it in already!"

I'm pleased to report that I refrained.

I was paid eight thousand dollars for that stellar performance, and I immediately took the money and bought a used Honda Civic to ease my nightmarish commute. Then I discovered how much it cost to park a car in Manhattan, and the Civic spent most of its time in front of my parents' place back in Connecticut.

The agency understood my situation, and did what it could to help. One Thursday I had a very early call, and the agency suggested I come into town and crash at one of its apartments. Until then, I didn't even know that it kept apartments for that very purpose. It was a perk for the more successful models. I was pleased. I figured it meant I was becoming one of the more successful models.

I went into Manhattan Wednesday night and found my way to the apartment. There was another model there, and I introduced myself and ran downstairs for some Heinekens. We shared a six-pack, then walked over to a happening club we'd been told about. We were from Click. We were models. Our names were on the List.

The club was loud and noisy and very crowded. I didn't drink anything in the club. I couldn't afford the drinks. That's why I'd had the Heinekens earlier. I made my way to the bar and asked for a glass of water, then wandered around, trying to find the courage to actually say hello to one of the dozens of gorgeous women in the place. I was still very shy.

I was studying one particularly attractive young lady when I began to feel very unsteady on my feet. I found my way to the men's room and almost blacked out. I had to sit on the floor for a minute, and I couldn't understand what had happened to the lights.

"You okay, man?"

I looked up. Somebody was talking to me, but I couldn't see him. "What happened to the power?" I said.

"What do you mean?"

Jesus. What was going on? Was I *blind*?

Somebody hollered for the guy and he took off and left me there. I struggled to my feet and groped my way outside, still blind. I had no idea what was happening. I knew it wasn't the beer—I'd built up plenty of tolerance to alcohol as a college student—so I began to wonder whether someone had slipped something into my drink. I was scared.

I groped my way toward the exit, hugging the walls, judging the route as best I could. The music was unbearably loud, I couldn't get oriented, and I began to panic.

"Michael?"

I recognized the voice. It was one of the bookers from Click. She asked if I was okay.

"I can't see," I said. "I'm fucking blind."

"Very funny," she said.

"I'm not screwing around."

She must have heard the panic in my voice. She took me by the hand and led me outside though the crush of bodies, then hailed a cab for the trip back to the apartment.

"What do you mean you can't see?" she asked me.

"I don't know. I can't see. My eyes are wide open and I can't see a goddamn thing."

"What are you on?"

"I'm not *on* anything," I said. "I don't do drugs."

"Michael," she said, a little more firmly this time. "Don't lie to me. I'm on your side. If you're on something, tell me what it is."

"You don't understand," I said, an edge creeping into my voice. "I'm not lying. I did pot once in my life and hated it."

"What have you been drinking then?"

"*Nothing.* I had three beers, an hour ago, and a single glass of water at the club. So either somebody slipped something into my water, or the club was pumping drugs through the vents."

She was clearly worried about me and decided to believe my story. The agencies take care of their own. I was one of Click's boys, and the staff had high hopes for me. But if I didn't work, they didn't make money. And—big surprise!—they were in it for the money. Don't get me wrong, I'm not saying that they didn't respond to me as a person. Then again, I'm not *not* saying it. Modeling is a business like any other business, only harsher and shallower.

"Are you feeling any better?"

"No," I said. "I still can't see a goddamn thing."

The cab pulled up outside the building. She paid the driver, took the keys from me and opened the door, and we went upstairs. It was a balmy night. She thought I'd be better off outdoors, in the fresh air, so she took me up to the roof and we sat and chatted and slowly my vision came back.

"You gave me a scare, Michael."

"*You?*" I said. "I gave *me* a scare."

Since we'd just been though a major drama together, she decided to get totally honest with me. She told me that the agency was very high on me. And it thought I had the goods. But also there was some concern about my unwillingness to move to New York. I was aware of this. I had been hearing it a lot lately. Bookers would call to see if I could take a job, but I was trapped in Connecticut and there was always a better than fifty-fifty chance that I wouldn't make it.

"Everyone respects your desire to finish college," she said, "and everyone thinks it's a very smart move on your part. But we're running a business here. The bookers are getting frustrated. They're tired of calling and hearing that you're not going to be able to make it. You have to make a decision, Michael."

Christ. What a great time to hit me with this shit. I knew too many guys who barely made it through high school. I'd seen what they did for a living, and I knew where they were going to be in five or ten years. They could have it. I wasn't criticizing; I wasn't passing judgment. But I didn't want to be one of those guys.

"I'm not going to drop out of college," I said. "I didn't put in three years for nothing. I'll make this happen. I *want* to make it happen. But don't tell me that I've been hitting the books for three years for nothing."

She didn't say anything.

"Trust me," I said. "I want this. And I'll work hard for it. But don't make me choose. I'm going to get my degree."

In the weeks and months ahead, I continued to work, on and off, as always. Small jobs mostly. But I stayed in school. And I continued to sense the agency's waning interest in me. But then something good would come along, and we'd be back on track. That summer, I did a job for Sizzle Sportswear. The owner liked my abs and gave me six hundred dollars for the privilege of using them in the advertising campaign. I did another gig for a store called Bradley's. I was up to seventy-five dollars an hour. The agency was happy with me. As far as Click was concerned, I was on the right track. It was still early in my career, sure, but that made it all the more significant. Click would make me a success.

Strangely, this made me a little nervous. I'd been nervous when I started, true, but that was because I hadn't known what to do. I figured I'd get more comfortable in front of the camera with time, but I was wrong. The nervousness never dissipated. Photographers would ask me for a certain look or a certain emotion, and I'd do my best to give it to them, but I always did it with a level of self-consciousness. I never learned to ignore the hot lights and the giant fans. And it all seemed so ridiculous. Run in place. Look angry. Look at me like you love me.

By the end of a shoot, I was usually a wreck. But somehow I managed. I began to book bigger and better jobs. Alas, instead of making me more confident, it filled me with more dread. Suddenly, there was more at stake. I was making money, and there was more to come. Thousands. Maybe *tens* of thousands. Not an occasional gig: a career. And the notion scared the shit out of me.

I was now only a month away from getting my B.A. The plan had always been to get that degree and find an entry-level job at a company with lots of promise. Then I'd find a modest place near home and remain close to my friends and family. It had been a good plan way back when. Now it didn't look like much of a plan. To be honest, it was unappealing in the extreme.

One Sunday, at dinner with the parents, I broke it to them. "I'm thinking of moving to New York," I said. "I'm going to try to get into this modeling thing full-time."

My mother didn't say much. She looked at my father.

"Well, you're not a kid anymore," my father said. "It's your life. If you've thought this through, and you really want to give it a shot, I'm not going to try to talk you out of it."

That was the thing about my father. It was obvious he didn't like the idea, but he wasn't going to ruin it for me. He would support me a hundred percent.

I graduated in May 1992, and stayed home for a month to hang with the family. But in late June I told one of my agents that I was looking for a part-time job—in *Manhattan*—and that as soon as I found one, I'd find a place to live and move there permanently. In short, I would never miss another casting call.

He called me back a few days later to say he had a job for me, as a doorman at the Paramount Hotel, on Forty-sixth Street between Broadway and Eighth. It was a haven for unemployed models. "You'll fit right in," he said.

"Great," I said, and I was on my way.

I drove into the city one Tuesday morning and went straight to the Paramount Hotel to get fitted for my uniform. I had a college degree and I was going to be opening doors for people. People who could afford to stay at this swanky place. And it *was* swanky. It was Ian Schrager's baby. Everything about it was hip and trendy and cool, though I didn't know anything about hip, trendy, or cool. I was barely out of my acid-washed jeans, remember?

I started work on a Sunday at seven o'clock in the morning, but my day began at four, behind the wheel of my little Honda. I'd be in the city by six, circling various blocks on the off-chance that I'd find a parking spot. It never happened. I always ended up in some high-priced lot. Then I'd hustle over to the hotel.

There wasn't much to the job. Open the door, greet the guest with a pleasant smile, close the door. My looks were opening a lot of doors. But not for me. And not a *lot* either. They were opening *one* door, for eight hours a day.

I left work at three and would pray for light traffic for the drive home. Once again, between gas and parking, the job was a losing proposition. But I hung in. Fighting sleep as I drove into town. Looking for parking. Opening the big glass doors. Smiling. Running out to greet every arriving cab and limo. Hustling over with the trolley. Hefting bags. Trying not to appear overly impressed by the celebrities. ("Oh my God! It's Chaka Kahn! And look, Weird Al Yankovic!") Okay, so they weren't that impressive. To *you*. But I'd seen these people on TV!

Toward the end of my first week, I met Sara, a girl who worked in the newsstand at the hotel. She said she'd heard I was looking for a place to live, and she had an apartment on the Upper East Side. I went to see it the following day. It was a two-bedroom, and I liked it, but I couldn't afford to split the fifteen-hundred dollar rent.

"The best I can do is four hundred," I told her. "And even that's going to be tough."

She called her daddy. Turned out he was helping with the rent. She told him about me and said I seemed like a nice guy, and he gave her the okay. I moved in the next day. I brought one duffel bag, filled with all my worldly possessions, and invested in a red futon.

Then I met Carolyn, and my life changed. That fateful night at

Joe's Café. The five-day wait for her phone call. The whirlwind romance. True love.

I thought she was it. My missing half. Girl of my dreams. It was the best month of my life, and it was the worst month of my life.

When I returned to New York after that weekend of licking my wounds in Naugatuck, I vowed to forget Carolyn. As far as I was concerned, she had never existed.

3.

Moving On

It is impossible to love and be wise.
—Francis Bacon, "Of Love," *Essays*

I got back to the Manhattan apartment and found my roommate, Sara, waiting up for me, watching TV. "I'm glad you're here," she said, reaching for the remote and killing the picture. "I found someone to take your room. I'll need you gone by Sunday."

Women. Go figure.

Suddenly I had to find a place to live. And I had no friends to speak of. I was back to being that lonely, lost kid in Manhattan, with an added burden: a broken heart. I had nothing to keep me going but hope. Even *false* hope.

Then I remembered Mitch Fraser, the photographer, and I dug out his phone number and dialed. I wasn't sure he'd remember me, but he remembered right away. I explained my situation and told him I needed a few days to look for a place of my own.

"No problem," he said. "When should I expect you?"

"How's Sunday morning?" I said.

"Fine," he said. "I'll see you then."

The week went by. Slowly. A week of opening and closing doors. A week of trying *not* to think about Carolyn (and failing miserably). A week of crying jags in the bathtub.

Then Sunday rolled around, and I packed up my red futon and my worldly possessions and snuck off before Sara got out of bed. I went downstairs and hailed a cab, tossed everything into the trunk, and rode down to Mitch's place. I rang the buzzer. No answer. I rang again. Still nothing. I was beginning to wonder whether this was my first day of homelessness when the door clicked open. I struggled up the stairs to the apartment. Mitch was waiting for me in the hallway. "I'm sorry," he said. "The doorbell's been shorting out."

I told him how happy I was to be there, that in all my months in New York City he was the only person who had been kind enough to reach out and offer a helping hand. He showed me around the apartment. It was small, a one-bedroom, but the couch pulled out into a bed.

"It's pretty comfortable," he said. "And if it's not comfortable enough, you can always crawl into bed with me." He was joking, of course. Or was he? I'd been a little worried about that. Mitch was clearly and openly gay. I hadn't had all that much experience with gays. I'd met a few of them in college, and there were plenty of them around every time I showed up for a shoot. But I couldn't say I really *knew* them.

"I think the couch will be fine," I said. I tried to say it casually, but Mitch saw the concern in my eyes.

"Relax," he said. "You have nothing to worry about. Put your things away. Make yourself at home."

"I'll be out of here in a week," I said. "Two at the most."

The following month, I got three gigs in a row. Nothing big, mind you, and nothing memorable, but real work, steady work. I decided that my days as a doorman were over, and I gave the folks at the Paramount two weeks' notice.

"Good luck," they said, but I could see they didn't mean it.

Mitch, on the other hand, was very happy for me. And very supportive. He took me out to dinner to celebrate my newfound freedom. By this time we had become friends. Real friends. One of my *only* friends, come to think of it, now that Carolyn had disappeared. We would go to movies together. Order in. Watch TV. Stop for a drink at a neighborhood bar or chow down at the cheap Chinese joint around the corner. He never came on to me. Not even when he'd had one beer too many. As a result, I was very relaxed around him. Still, there were times when I found Mitch looking at me longingly, and I knew that deep down inside he still hoped I'd come around. That gay vibe was still out there, and some of his gay friends probably assumed we were together.

One morning, shortly after I left the Paramount, I got a fateful call from Click about a gig for Calvin Klein. Well, not Calvin exactly; it was for his wife, Kelly. She had just finished a book about swimming pools, one of those expensive coffee-table tomes, and she was celebrating by throwing a party at a swanky Manhattan penthouse with a rooftop swimming pool. Kelly wanted to hire five guys to wander around the pool in nothing but their underwear. They were supposed to look like lifeguards, only more perfect and more ravishing. The job paid three hundred dollars.

This was around September 1992, if I remember correctly. I didn't want to do it—I knew there was a pretty good chance I'd run into Carolyn—but I didn't have much choice. It was a job. It could lead to other jobs. And I needed the money.

So that's how I found myself traipsing around a chic Manhattan pool party in my Calvin Klein underwear, along with four other hunks of beef. We were ornaments—just there to look pretty and scrumptious. It was humiliating. Then again, what was I whining about? That's what models *did*. That's what they were *for*. What had I expected? That someone would actually mistake me for a human being?

And then, just as I'd feared, there she was, coming through the front door, and slowly working her way through the crowded room. My heart began beating like crazy. I tried to keep my distance—tried to keep the pool between us—but I'd already seen her looking at me. I watched her now as she began to inch her way over, pausing here and there to kiss someone hello.

I was so embarrassed I thought I'd implode.

"How are you, Michael?" she asked.

I looked into her eyes and fell in love all over again.

"Good," I said. I tried to say it hard, tried to show a little anger, a little coldness. But I didn't feel any anger or any coldness. I felt *longing*.

"You look great," she said, looking around. She had obligations to fulfill as a publicist, and talking to me for any length of time might have struck some people as unseemly. "Can we chat later?"

"Sure," I said, but I didn't get my hopes up. She moved off and I watched her go. I felt like a wimp, like at the very least I should have copped a little attitude.

Suddenly, there was a commotion near the front door, and I saw the photographers trampling one another in their haste to get there. JFK Jr. had just arrived. He smiled and posed gamely for pictures. He posed for a shot with Calvin. He posed again with Kelly. He posed a third time with both Calvin and Kelly. People, mostly women, stared.

Then John Jr. broke away and crossed the room, and I noticed Carolyn standing discreetly off to one side, quietly watching. She smiled at him; he leaned close and kissed her on the cheek. Okay. Fine. It was nothing. We live in a kissy society. They were just friends. Really. Why was it bothering me anyway? Carolyn and I were history. Still, there was something there that bothered me: she and John Jr. had that same easy familiarity I'd noticed back at Joe's Café, when Carolyn spoke to Jason at the bar. Clearly there was more to this relationship than Carolyn had admitted.

At that moment, almost as if she could hear my thoughts, she turned and caught me watching her from across the distance. Then John Jr. leaned in for a quick kiss and hurried toward the door, with the paparazzi once again hot on his tail.

Shortly thereafter, the party broke up. I got dressed, headed out, and found Carolyn waiting for me by the elevators.

"Hey," I said, trying to look unsurprised.

"Hey," she said back as she joined me in the elevator.

We rode down in silence, stepped out of the building, and headed south. It was a cool night, but I felt warm, and my heart was beating fast again.

"So how's your buddy John Jr.?" I asked. I knew it was a shitty thing to say, but I was hurting. I was a fucking cabana boy; he was a goddamn prince.

"Why are you still going on about him?" she said, and with genuine tenderness. "I told you. He's not my type. He's not for me. I'm not interested in him or the life he leads."

I wasn't sure I believed it. John Jr. was the most eligible bachelor in the world. Maybe she wasn't lying. Maybe the weekend at Martha's Vineyard hadn't gone all that well. Maybe she wanted him but he didn't want her. I was torturing myself into a lousy mood, and she could see it. "Michael," she said. "Can we just drop it? Please?"

"How come you never called me back?" I asked, trying to keep the pain out of my voice.

"I don't know," she said.

"I must have called a hundred times."

"I didn't exactly get the royal treatment when I went to see you at the Paramount," she said. "Remember?"

I remembered, all right. But I remembered it differently. I remembered her pissiness, the snarl in her voice. It had felt, even then, as if she had some kind of agenda. I'm not sure what it was exactly, but I suspected she was out to sabotage the relationship. Although I didn't know why. I didn't understand it that day at the hotel, and I sure didn't understand it now. I found myself becoming increasingly confused. If it had been her intent to dump me, why didn't she just tell me it was over? And if it was over, why had she been waiting for me by the elevators?

More important, what were we doing now? And where were we going?

"You make me crazy," I said.

We ended up at her place. We were hungry for each other and it was over fast. Too fast.

"Meow," she said after we made love.

"Meow," I replied, drifting off.

It was this silly little thing we used to do. We'd cuddle up and meow at each other, usually in bed, varying the tone and inflection to communicate our feelings. Carolyn could put a lot of love into her meows. I think she found conveying her emotions through meowing to be a lot easier than speaking about them.

Come morning she had to rush off to work—no time for that bagel with tomatoes—and we went our separate ways. I didn't hear from her that day or the next, and I didn't think it was my place to call her. On the third day, I realized I probably wouldn't hear from her again. And I accepted it. It was easy to rationalize. She was too much for me; I wasn't in her league. And if she didn't want me, what was the point? I wasn't going to beg.

So I tried to forget her. And the steady gigs helped. That fall, every other weekend I went home to see my family. To hang out with my buddies. To get a home-cooked meal. Anything to actively *not* think about Carolyn.

It was during one of these visits that I ran into Rachel Critelli again. She had just broken up with her boyfriend, and I was still quietly pining for Carolyn. We were a perfect match. We went home together. That weekend and the two that followed.

"So are we dating again or what?" she asked one Sunday morning as I was getting ready to head back to the city.

"I guess," I said.

That's how we did things in small-town Naugatuck. We defined them. We felt more secure knowing exactly who we were and what was expected of us. We liked labels. And the truth is, I didn't think there was anything wrong with labels. I liked knowing that Rachel was my girlfriend, and I liked being able to refer to her, publicly and privately, as my girlfriend. We had nothing to hide, nothing to worry about. I had nothing to prove.

As time passed, it felt increasingly *right*. Rachel and I had grown up in the same town, and we were from very similar backgrounds. I began to feel that we really belonged together. It was great coming up every other weekend to see her and the gang and our families. We spent Thanksgiving together, then Christmas. We celebrated the New Year with all our old friends and made plans to go to Jamaica with her sister and her boyfriend and three other couples a few months later.

I forgot all about Carolyn.

But in early March, a couple weeks before the trip to Jamaica, I was back in Manhattan and the phone rang. It was Carolyn. She said she wanted to see me and wondered if she could stop by and visit. I hung up and waited for her to arrive. Her timing struck me as unreal. Was she psychic? Did she know I was seeing Rachel again? I wondered what the hell she wanted from me.

The buzzer rang, she walked in, meowed, and kissed me. We made love.

"Why do you do this to me?" I whispered as we drifted off to sleep.

"I don't know," she said.

The better question would have been why I had allowed it to happen. I was seeing Rachel again, and I felt lousy. But clearly not lousy enough to stop it. There was an addictive quality to my relationship with Carolyn that neither of us had the strength or willpower to resist.

I woke up at two in the morning to find her gathering her clothes and getting dressed. "Where are you going?" I said.

"I have a busy day ahead of me."

"Does your day always start this early?"

She smiled at me in that way of hers—*Let's not go there*—then finished getting dressed, kissed me on the lips, and left. I guess she was going home to someone else. Why else leave at that ungodly hour?

The phone woke me later that morning. It was Rachel. She was wondering if I was coming up that weekend, our last weekend before Jamaica. I said I wasn't sure; I'd let her know. I hung up and felt terrible. I had just cheated on Rachel, with whom I was about to get on a plane for a romantic weekend. Rachel, my girlfriend. I lay back against the pillows and could still smell the Egyptian Musk on the sheets. I felt even worse. Why was Carolyn doing this to me? Didn't she know how it would affect me? Or maybe that was the whole point: she *did* know. I felt like an alcoholic must feel when he falls off the wagon. *Okay, I screwed up. But it was just one little drink. I can beat this thing.*

I told myself once more that I wouldn't call Carolyn again. If she didn't call, she'd never hear from me again. And I was fine with that. I had a girlfriend.

I didn't hear from her of course, but it was just as well. I was going to make things work with Rachel. We had a future together.

So off we went to Jamaica, Rachel and I and our little entourage.

We drank all the way to Kingston, landed with a buzz, then took a van to the resort. It was a beautiful place. Azure waters, sandy beaches, a cooling breeze, cozy cabins right on the water. Everyone had a wonderful first day. Everyone except Rachel and me.

"What's wrong?" I asked.

"Nothing," she said.

But something *was* wrong. It was the most romantic place I'd ever been in my life, but the romance didn't appear to be working on Rachel. We were there for nine days and only made love twice, and without much enthusiasm from her on either occasion. I didn't understand what was happening to us. I suddenly found myself thinking about Carolyn.

Rachel and I gimped through the last few days, barely speaking, then we found ourselves back in New York, at the baggage carousel, waiting for our luggage. She was getting on a bus back to Connecticut, and I was heading directly into the city. But I wanted to know what was up before we parted ways. I saw my bag rocking toward us on the noisy carousel.

"Rachel," I said, taking her aside. "We were just on a beautiful island for what was supposed to be a romantic getaway, and I've never felt so removed from anyone in my life. You want to tell me what's wrong?"

"I don't know what's wrong," she said. "Nothing's wrong. Everything's wrong."

"Then what's the point of staying together?" I asked.

She looked at me, as if to say there wasn't any point, and her eyes filled with tears.

"That's it?" I said, hoping she'd say something magical—something that would make everything better. But Rachel didn't say anything. She half shrugged and shook her head.

So I turned, grabbed my bag, and took off without another look in her direction. I didn't even say good-bye to the others. I hopped in a cab to Manhattan, feeling crushed and disconnected and very, very lonely.

Two days later, as fate would have it, I found myself at Calvin Klein for a general meeting with the casting team. One of the assistants spotted me in the waiting room and went out back to tell Carolyn. A few moments later, Carolyn herself came out to say hello. She looked gorgeous.

"What's wrong?" she said. Those were the first words out of her mouth, followed by "You look miserable." She knew me that well; she could see right through me. And she got the whole crazy story out of me, right there in the lobby: Rachel. Jamaica. The coldness. That entire painful week.

She knew about Rachel—I had mentioned her once or twice, albeit briefly—and she was surprised that we were dating again. She also seemed bothered by the fact that the troubles with Rachel had affected me so deeply. Maybe she was jealous: *How dare another woman cause you pain! That's my job.* Or maybe she was hurt: *How quickly you found someone to replace me!*

But I'm just guessing here, and guessing wildly. I really don't know what she was thinking. I didn't then and I don't now. It's hard to get into anyone's head, and Carolyn's head was tougher than most. But whatever it was, she was there for me. It was surreal. I was sitting in the lobby of the Calvin Klein offices, waiting to see the casting team, talking to a woman who had recently broken my heart about a second woman who had broken my heart even *more* recently, and damn if I didn't begin to cry.

Fortunately, I got called to my meeting, and I was forced to pull myself together. Carolyn wished me luck, and I thanked her for listening to me and for letting me cry on her shoulder.

"I'll call you," she said.

I went in to see the casting director. Nothing much happened. *Looking good. Love your portfolio.* Then I went back to the apartment and waited for Carolyn's call. But she didn't call. Not that day. Not the next day. And not the day after that.

But on the third day the phone rang and she asked me to join her and a friend for drinks. *A friend?* This was unusual in the extreme. The friend turned out to be Gordon Henderson, a designer who had worked briefly at Calvin Klein. He had since moved on to launch his own line, and *People* magazine had recently dubbed him one of the fifty Most Beautiful People in the World. Gordon didn't let it go to his head. Not much anyway. I liked him. He was black and gay and warm and a little outrageous, and always fun to be around. I'd have to say that Gordon was probably Carolyn's closest friend. And, in the months ahead, we became close too.

He was also one of the few people who figured out that there was more to my relationship with Carolyn than met the eye. He could sense that there was history there, and he suspected there was more to come. But for the time being Carolyn and I were concentrating on making it as friends. And I was okay with that. It was better than not having her in my life.

This went on for weeks on end. Carolyn would call at the last minute and we'd hook up at a bar or a club or a restaurant and hang out. On many occasions, she was there in an official capacity, representing Calvin Klein, and she had to work the room. So I hung out, made small talk with the other guests and patrons. "Michael Bergin. A model. Carolyn? She's just a friend. A good friend."

And it was true too. She *was* a friend, a *good* friend. She was taking care of me. Nursing me back to health, emotionally speaking. Still, it wasn't quite that simple. I guess it never is. Carolyn would always light up when she saw me, literally glowing from within. And I always felt electrified when I saw her. Every time she leaned in for that hello kiss on the cheek, she left me hungering for more. But how could I tell her that? She had successfully redefined the relationship. We were in a place that felt safe to her. Who was I to screw it up?

Ironically, she kept asking about Rachel, analyzing my relationship with her, curious about every aspect of it. I don't know what she hoped to learn from it, but I think she was still troubled by my tears. I had never cried for her; not that she'd seen anyway. I think Carolyn would have liked that; I suspect she wanted to be loved with that kind of intensity.

"I don't think Rachel realizes how lucky she is to be loved like that," she told me one evening, still obsessing. Suddenly I remembered the night she had cried after we made love. "This is too good," she had said. "I'm too happy. I don't want this to end." And when I told her it didn't have to end, she had replied, chillingly, "Everything ends."

Maybe *that's* what this was about. Carolyn wanted guarantees in love. She wanted to know that it was forever. Anything short of that just wasn't good enough. Maybe that's why she'd been reluctant to define our relationship as a relationship. Relationships end, after all. And maybe that's why she found it so hard to commit. Not just to me, but to anyone. She'd rather have *friends,* as she called them. Friends come and go; friendships are less noisy, less demanding, and, consequently, less frightening.

I decided to go out into the world and meet new people and make friends of my own. One of these friends was Vince Young, a fellow model, also repped by Click. He shared a SoHo apartment with three other models, and he called one night to invite me to a party. I like parties, but I'm shy, and I often find myself standing around, feeling awkward. And this was no different. I stood around for an hour, feeling as awkward as ever, and—just as I was about to leave—the front door opened and in walked two beautiful blondes. I told myself, *Michael, there are two of them. Go on. Say something witty. There's a chance one of them will respond.*

But they weren't alone. They were with a guy, *one* guy, but he happened to be Jack Nicholson. Apparently, one of the models who lived in the apartment was taking acting classes, and his teacher was tight with Jack. Jack was grinning his trademark grin, and trying to act like a regular guy, but he couldn't pull it off. There was something electric about him. It was as if he had single-handedly changed the molecular structure of the room. It struck me that what I'd heard about certain celebrities was true: they had It, whatever the hell It was. Star power isn't a myth; it is tangible and forceful.

Jack and the girls sat down and had a drink, and people tried not to stare. Some of them succeeded, I guess, but I couldn't keep my eyes off him. I wanted to shake his hand so I could tell people about it later. But I was terrified. *That's Jack Nicholson over there. I am in a room with Jack Nicholson.*

Still, I really wanted this. And I figured I'd better get to it before the opportunity slipped away. I took a deep breath and walked over, feeling like a big, nervous kid, dizzy with excitement. I looked him in the eye and said, "Hi, pleased to meet you. I'm Jack Nicholson."

And he looked up at me and did that thing he does with his eyebrows and grinned his grin and said, "Really? I thought *I* was Jack Nicholson."

Everyone laughed. It was the biggest laugh I ever got. And no one laughed louder than Jack.

I told Gordon the story a few nights later, when we were out with Carolyn. They laughed too. Gordon liked me. And he liked to mess with Carolyn about us. He'd say, "What are you waiting for, girl? Look at this hunk of man. He's perfect. Packages don't get much better than this."

Carolyn would smile good-naturedly, but I think it made her

nervous. Gordon had figured out our history—he was one of the few—and genuinely believed that Carolyn and I belonged together. Oddly enough, I was slowly getting used to the idea that it was never going to happen. I *thought* I was anyway. I kept telling myself to be realistic, that Carolyn was way out of my league. The way she handled herself. The way she handled other people. Her education. The books she read. The foreign films I'd never heard of. She was a smart, cultured, beautiful, sexy woman. Too much for me.

As I grew to accept this, or *thought* I grew to accept it, thanks to the miracle of self-denial, we became closer than ever. Sometimes it would be the three of us—Carolyn, Gordon, and I—hitting the clubs. The Tunnel. The Sound Factory. Les Deux. Tunnel. Dinner at Odeon. Sometimes it was just Carolyn and me, hooking up at the last minute for a bite to eat or keeping each other company at some work-related event.

It was very comfortable, and it was also very *superficial*. Carolyn and I were careful to keep things fun and impersonal. I never asked whether she was seeing anyone, and she didn't pry into my life. Not that I had a life. I hadn't been with anyone since Rachel in Jamaica, and—as you may recall—that hadn't been particularly good.

On occasion, when the nights got a little long, there were drugs. I dabbled from time to time, but I didn't seem to have the constitution for it. As for Carolyn, the stories about her rampant drug use are patently untrue. There was drug use, yes, but it was modest. No, actually, that's wrong: in Carolyn's case, it was *minimal*. I mean, think about it: Carolyn was all about self-control. Her job was all about appearances. Does it really make any sense that she would risk letting herself go? I never saw Carolyn looking "hollow-eyed" or "coked up," despite reports to the contrary, and I don't know anyone who did.

Finding my own place didn't quite work out as planned. In May 1993, Mitch moved to a two-bedroom place on Twentieth Street, and I went with him. He paid the majority of the rent, and I paid what I could afford. And I could actually afford a little more now. I'd done a number of catalogue shoots and a few newspaper inserts—in my underwear, capitalizing on those hard-earned abs—and I was getting a little promotional work from some smaller outfits. I wouldn't call it a career yet, but I was trying to be optimistic.

Mitch and I would hang out together. He still wanted me in his bed, and he joked about it, sometimes pretty brazenly, but it didn't faze me. I was comfortable around him. I was comfortable around Gordon. I was comfortable around all the gay fashionistas who surrounded me in those days. And I was comfortable because I knew it was never going to go beyond friendship. I wasn't interested in men or dogs or inflatable dolls; I was interested in women.

Although I'm not the smoothest operator on the block. I'm not that aggressive. And I'm not too good with the one-liners. ("Hi. I couldn't help noticing you.") And in any event, that's not who I am or how I operate. I like sex as much as the next person, but sex without emotion leaves me feeling empty. I don't like coming and running; it tells me I just had sex with the wrong woman. On the other hand, I hadn't been laid in a while, and I *was* getting horny, if not downright desperate. And that's when I saw her. . . .

I was at Café Tabac, a little place on Ninth Street, having a beer. She was shooting pool at the solitary table by the bar. She was small and perfectly proportioned, and she was wearing a snug little sundress that showed off all her curves. She noticed me noticing her, and she smiled and made it easy for me. So I went over and put a quarter on the pool table.

"Hey," I said with my usual opening-line flair. "I'm Michael."

"Nicole," she said—at least that's what I'll refer to her as.

She joined me for a beer after her game. She was really beautiful and easy to talk to. She was also quick to inform me that she had recently broken things off with her boyfriend, and that she was in no rush to get involved again. Still, she seemed to like me. And before the evening ended she gave me her phone number.

I called her the next day. We hooked up. "Want to see where I work?" she asked. "Sure," I said. I thought it was a little strange, but I went along. Then it got stranger: she took me to Platinum, a strip club.

"This is where you work?" I asked.

"Uh-huh," she said. She looked into my face for a reaction. What was I going to say? With a body like that, why not?

I had only been to one strip club in my life, back in Connecticut, and I had been seriously underwhelmed. The women weren't much to look at, and the place stank of piss and stale beer. But Platinum occupied the other end of the spectrum. It was a very classy place, and all of the women were almost as gorgeous as Nicole. We had a drink and watched a couple of her friends dance. They were nice to look at, but I felt kind of sorry for them. I wondered if their mothers knew what they did for a living.

"You going to dance?" I asked Nicole.

"No," she said. "I'm off tonight. And I wouldn't feel comfortable dancing in front of you."

"Why?"

"Because I think I like you. A little."

"It would be different if you didn't like me?"

"Completely different," she said. "I wouldn't care."

I think she liked me more than a little. Before we left the club, she invited me to spend the following weekend at the Jersey shore, at the home of one of her girlfriend's. I accepted.

The next night I got a call from Carolyn. She told me she was hungry and would I meet her for a sandwich. So we met near her place and I told her about Nicole. I didn't see why I should keep it from her—Carolyn was a friend, after all, a *good* friend—and I was pretty excited about the upcoming weekend. I even described Nicole in great detail: small, voluptuous, exotic, half Filipino, smart and funny too.

Suddenly Carolyn seemed really bothered. She stopped picking at her food; she stopped picking at mine even. She looked deflated, as if all the air had been let out of her.

"What's wrong?" I asked.

"Nothing," she said. "I'm tired."

But I could see it had nothing to do with being tired. This business with Nicole was really bugging her. Now I began to wonder why I'd said anything at all, and whether my subconscious was playing games with me. Had it been deliberate? Was I trying to hurt her? Did I want to make her jealous?

"Tell me the truth," I said. "What is it, really?"

She looked at me with disgust and said, "I can't believe you'd go out with a stripper."

"Carolyn—"

But she cut me off. She was tired, she repeated. She wanted to get the hell home. She barked for the waiter, I paid, and we left. She wouldn't even talk to me on the way home. She didn't even kiss me good night at the door.

Friday night I went out to Jersey with Nicole. We had the place to ourselves. It was small and comfortable, though not as spectacular as I'd imagined it. We made love for the first time. It was nice. I didn't feel like running away afterward.

The next morning, as we lazed over breakfast, the phone rang. It was Nicole's ex-boyfriend. He had heard about me—probably from one of the strippers—and he was on his way to Jersey to kill me. Nicole hung up, but he called back and she let the phone ring.

"We better cut this short," she said.

"Why?" I said. "You really think he'll kill me?"

"I don't know about kill you," she said, "but he's a real psycho, and he'll probably go for serious damage."

Serious damage? I could live without it. We left.

We held hands on the train back to New York. We kissed a little. Nicole told stories about her childhood, about how nervous she was the first time she danced. "I have the body of a stripper and the soul of a homemaker," she told me. "I'd like to live in a quiet suburb and have a husband with a boring job, two cute kids, and a medium-sized SUV that gets pretty good gas mileage."

She was funny. I liked her.

The following Wednesday, I hooked up with Carolyn and Gordon at the Sound Factory. Carolyn asked about my "dirty" weekend. She was smiling, and I couldn't see beyond the smile to the pain inside, so I told her all about it. I told her about the crazy ex-boyfriend. And I told her about the ride back to New York. And I told her that I really liked Nicole, and that I was serious about pursuing a relationship. "Maybe I'm just on the rebound from Rachel," I added. "I don't know. And I'm a little worried, frankly. She's not the type of girl you bring home to mom."

Carolyn had been listening intently, but now she stood abruptly and disappeared in the direction of the restrooms. I looked over at Gordon. He was shaking his head from side to side.

"What?" I said.

"Don't you see *anything*?" he asked.

"What do you mean?"

"You're not on the rebound from Rachel, you fool. You're on the rebound from Carolyn. And Carolyn can't see what's in front of her either. She wants you too, but she won't acknowledge it."

"How can you say that?" I protested.

"Open your eyes, Michael. You're going on and on about your

little stripper, and Carolyn's smiling and nodding at all the right places. But any fool can see she's all broken up inside. Any fool but you."

"You're wrong," I said. "Carolyn and I are finished. She finished it."

"What?" he said. "You think women are logical? Where emotions are concerned, *none* of us is logical."

Carolyn returned from the ladies' room. She seemed restless, wired. "Let's go," she said, but she was addressing only me, not Gordon. "I need you to drop me at home."

We said good-bye to Gordon and left him there. The minute we were outside we jumped in a cab, and she told me she was very upset with me.

"About Nicole?" I asked. I felt kind of thick. I didn't really believe what Gordon had told me, even though a small part of me must have wanted to believe it.

"Yes," she said. "About Nicole. And about everything else. I don't know why it bothers me, but it bothers me. A lot. And I hate it."

I didn't know how to respond to that. I didn't know what to think. So I blurted out the first thing that was in my head. "Gordon thinks that I'm not over you," I said.

"What do you think?" she said.

"I think he might be right."

When we reached her place, I paid the driver and we got out. I could see she wanted to invite me up, but she didn't. She looked sad and lost. "I'll call you," she said.

"You okay?"

"Sure," she said, though clearly she wasn't, and she turned and went inside.

I walked on, alone, my mind reeling. Carolyn really *was* upset about Nicole, and I didn't know what to make of it. I had come to accept the fact that our relationship was over, and if I began to believe otherwise I felt I'd only be torturing myself.

When I got back to the apartment—Mitch was out of town again—the phone rang. It was Carolyn. "What are you doing?" she asked.

"Nothing," I said.

"Can I come over?"

She came over. She walked in the door and she held me and kissed me and the next thing I knew we were taking off each other's clothes.

"Meow," she said.

"I've missed you too," I said.

And just like that, we were back.

It was as if we had never been apart. And the same rules applied. Our relationship, if we chose to call it that, was vague and ill-defined. No labels. No plans. She'd call when she could call; we'd get together when it was feasible (for her). I felt like "the girl": like I was supposed to sit quietly by the phone, willing it to ring, and hoping to hear from her. And it was important that I not make any unreasonable demands. But the odd thing is that it didn't bother me. I was just happy to have her back in my life and not just as a good friend. I wasn't going to let myself get jealous. I wasn't going to suffocate her. And we were always together anyway. We saw each other every day, so I never got a chance to miss her.

I couldn't get enough of those blue eyes. I loved the way she clung to me at night, loved the way she always pushed me off the edge of the bed. I loved the way she leapt to her feet in the morning and got herself ready in seven minutes flat. I loved the way her voice sounded on the phone. I loved the way she ordered me around: "Nine o'clock. Odeon. Don't be late."

★ ★ ★

One midsummer night, we were lying in her bed in a postcoital haze, and she told me that my eyebrows were too thick. She went off to get the tweezers, and I, in bed, my head in her lap, let her pluck away. When she was done, I got up to take a leak and saw my reflection in the mirror. I was a little taken aback. My brows had been reduced to two small lines. "Wow," I called out to her. "I look like Linda Evangelista."

She laughed. I left the bathroom and rejoined her in bed. "You look great," she said.

"Are you sure?" I said. "You don't think you got a little carried away?"

"Not at all," she said.

The next day, I had a fitting for a Levi's campaign. I was pretty excited. Levi's jeans, and the photographer was Albert Watson. Way cool. When I arrived for the fitting, the client took one look at my eyebrows, and her jaw dropped.

"What's wrong?" I asked.

"You look like a girl," she said. She went off to call my agency to cancel me. I was understandably upset, and I called my agency to complain. But I couldn't get three words in. The agency was too busy reaming me: "What the hell were you thinking, Michael?! What the hell did you do to your eyebrows?!"

I went over to Carolyn's that night. "Guess what?" I said, whining. "Levi's canceled me. They said I looked like a girl!"

"Oh, honey," Carolyn said. "I'm so sorry." And suddenly she laughed. A big, gut-busting laugh. And I laughed too. That was Carolyn. My Carolyn. I could never be mad at her for long.

I was in love again. More deeply than ever. Every love song was about us. Every love story was our story. Carolyn was back.

"Heard from your *voluptuous* little stripper lately?" she asked me one night, punctuating the question with a laugh.

"No," I said.

"Miss her?"

"No."

It didn't bother me. Carolyn was allowing her insecurity to show, and it was actually sort of flattering. She was making it clear that she didn't want to lose me. What could be better?

One fine morning, at her place, we woke up late and she had to rush off. So I stayed and slept for another hour, finally stumbling out of bed and puttering around the tiny kitchen, looking for the coffee filters. I didn't find them, but I found something else under the kitchen sink. It was a copy of *People* magazine, stashed out of sight. John Jr. was on the cover; the Sexiest Man Alive. It was really bizarre. The issue was almost five years old—it dated back to 1988—and she'd hidden it away.

What the hell was going on?

My first impulse was to call Carolyn at work and confront her. But then I thought about it and realized that it was none of my business. So she went to Martha's Vineyard with John Jr. So what? I hadn't even known her then. So maybe they'd even slept together. What was I going to do about that? Maybe she got a kick out of seeing his face on the cover of *People*. How was this my business?

It wasn't quite as easy as I'm making it sound, but I managed to get myself under control. Then I did something I'm very proud of. I called her and asked her to come to Naugatuck with me to meet my family.

"Your family?" she said, wary.

"Yes," I said. "You'll love them."

"What brought this on?" she asked.

I could almost hear myself saying, *Well, you know, I found this copy of* People *magazine under your kitchen sink, with John Jr. on the cover. And he's not only the Sexiest Man Alive, but the World's Most Eligible*

Bachelor. And I know you have some nebulous history together, and I've been wondering about it, and frankly I'm more than a little freaked out.

Fortunately, I didn't say any of that. Generally speaking, I have good impulse control. "I just want you to meet my family," I said. "No agenda. I think they're great, and I think you'll think they're great."

"Can I get back to you on this?" she asked, being her usual non-committal self.

"Of course," I said. "Let me know."

She called me back an hour later and said she couldn't make it, so I went up alone. The next time I went to visit, same thing: Carolyn said she had things to do in the city. But two weeks later, with another weekend looming, she began to freak. She didn't want me to go up. Why couldn't I just stay with her? Why did we have to be apart for an entire weekend?

"I feel like you're always abandoning me," she whined. "I have separation anxiety." She was trying to make a little joke out of it, but clearly it wasn't a joke.

"Just come, then," I said. "We don't have to be apart."

"Okay," she said. And, just like that, we were on. But she got a look on her face: that worried Carolyn look. She asked me if I was supposed to be her boyfriend or something. (That commitment thing again.) And I said, "You can be anything you want to be, Carolyn. Why don't you just go as Carolyn Bessette?"

"Okay," she said. "Deal."

I called my parents, told them I was bringing her up, and asked them not to make a big deal over her. Not that they would've, but you know how parents are. My mother was always curious about the women in my life. She was always eager to meet them. She said she wanted to be able to visualize us together. But the funny thing is, none of the girls I ever brought home had been good enough for

Mom. She never said anything bad about any of them, and she was never rude or unkind, but I could see in her eyes that every last one of them fell short of expectations.

So in late June of 1993 Carolyn and I took the train to Naugatuck. When we arrived at this little blip of a town, the town where I'd grown up, my father was at the station, waiting for us. He was very pleasant—asked us about the ride up, talked about the weather—and then we were at the house. The house with the blue siding, the deck out back, and the aboveground pool. And my mother came out to say hello and she just lit up. Carolyn had that effect on people. She could electrify a room. She had a little of the It that Jack Nicholson exuded.

And I could see the look in my mother's eye. She was studying Carolyn, sizing her up, discreetly, the way women do, appraising her with those looks, and seeing a mature, sophisticated, articulate woman. A *real* woman. The first real woman I'd ever brought home. And I could see she was bowled over.

And I'll tell you: the whole weekend was a lovefest. Everybody in my family was just enamored of Carolyn. My parents, my brother, my two sisters, both my grandmothers—they all just fell madly in love with her.

I remember Carolyn in our living room, sitting on the L-shaped couch with her hand on my mother's arm. She had this thing about touching people. And she was already calling her Lorraine, and telling her how beautiful she was, how happy she was to be there, and of course she didn't forget to tell her what a great son she had.

My mother looked at me and she was beaming. It was as if she couldn't believe that this beautiful, classy, cultured, educated, well-spoken woman was with her lug of a son. I loved it.

Later, we went out and hooked up with some of my friends, many of them people I'd known since childhood, and they loved her too. Carolyn had a knack for putting people at ease. And she was also deeply focused. She would ask people about themselves, and she'd actually listen to the reply. She was genuinely interested. She'd look you right in the eye, and people found that very seductive. Part of that came from the fact that Carolyn didn't like to talk about herself, being intensely private, and she must have found it easier to listen to others than to talk about her own life. It worked like a charm. Most people are pretty self-absorbed; they love talking about themselves.

In short, my family and friends couldn't get enough of her. They joked that they didn't understand what she saw in a guy like me, though perhaps it wasn't such a joke after all.

We spent the night on the two wings of the L-shaped couch in the living room, which didn't give us much privacy—and that was exactly the point. My parents are a little old-fashioned. When I'm under their roof, I'm expected to play by their rules.

Sunday morning we were up and about, having breakfast together, one big happy family, and we soon discovered that even the family *bird,* Sammy, liked Carolyn. It was one of those sun conures with a short body, a long tail, and bright tropical feathers. And it was a very unfriendly bird. It bit most people, the two exceptions being my mother and me. Carolyn went up for a closer look at the bird, and I was about to warn her not to get too close, when it hopped on her shoulder and took to her like a love-struck puppy. The damn thing wouldn't leave her alone. When I went to reach for it, it pecked at me. Little bastard. This was the same bird that used to sleep under my shirt at night, and suddenly it wanted nothing to do with me. It was pressed up against Carolyn's throat, purring like a cat. That was the end of my relationship with that goddamn bird.

And then the weekend was over, and we were on the train back to New York. The whole way home Carolyn talked about how much she loved my family, how great they were, and how lucky I was. She said my father epitomized everything a father should be: solid, respectful, dependable, decent, supportive. But the way she was going on and on about him, I actually got a little jealous. It sounded like she had a crush on my old man.

It was odd. On our way up to Naugatuck, I had worried about her reaction to my family. I knew she came from wealthier stock, from a far more cultured world, and I was self-conscious about my comparatively modest roots. But she had nothing but nice things to say about them, and about all my friends, and the experience brought us closer than ever. She had seen another side of me, and I guess it made her feel as if she knew me a little better. Maybe she even liked what she was seeing.

After that trip, I felt pretty good, both personally and professionally. For a while there, and throughout the entire summer, I seemed unstoppable. I was getting more and more work, and I was actually beginning to make a few bucks. I still got nervous in front of the camera—I didn't think that that was ever going to change—but I was getting better at it. I was learning how to take direction.

"Look at me like you love me," one photographer told me. It felt a little strange, but I shot him a smoldering look, and he actually got a little flustered.

Another guy spent the whole shoot asking me to pretend I was a discus thrower in the Olympics. I tossed an imaginary discus in unimaginable ways. And still another guy had me playing air guitar throughout the session. It was ridiculous. I did "Stairway to Heaven" so many times that I even began to belt out the words: "Woe oh oh oh oh oh, and she's buying a stairway to heaven."

What can I say? That's showbiz, folks.

Then I got a "normal" job: I shot a Calvin Klein ad for Bloomingdale's, with Kate Moss, who was already a major superstar, that was to appear in the Sunday *New York Times*. I wasn't up to billboard standards yet, but it was a pretty big deal. Kate looked hot, and I looked hot. Even *I* thought I looked hot, which was something of a miracle. My agency definitely agreed, and eventually the people at Calvin Klein came around too.

Back in those days, Marky Mark, aka Mark Wahlberg, was the Calvin Klein underwear guy. But one night in L.A. he got into a brawl with Madonna and her entourage, and suddenly all this shit about his past began to surface: that he'd once robbed and assaulted two Vietnamese guys, that he was known to make racial slurs, that he had a hair-trigger temper. The bad publicity cost him his job at Calvin Klein, and the company began to look for a new underwear guy. All the agencies were scrambling to land the gig, and portfolios were raining down on CK from every corner of the known universe. But no one seemed to measure up.

At one point, Calvin changed tactics. He thought he might be better served by an established celebrity, and he considered people like Brad Pitt, Woody Harrelson, and even Anthony Kiedis of the Red Hot Chili Peppers. That didn't work out either, so CK was back to the models.

I got a call from Click in late September. "Guess what?" the agent said.

"What?"

"You're in the running."

"For what?"

"The Calvin Klein underwear campaign."

"I didn't even know I'd been submitted," I said. It was true, I didn't. I didn't even consider myself in that league. And, no, this isn't false modesty. The truth is, when I wake up in the morning and look in the mirror, I only see the flaws.

By this time, Carolyn was coming up to Naugatuck with me almost every other weekend. She'd become family. And suddenly, from one visit to the next, the house rules changed: my parents let us have a bedroom to ourselves. We didn't talk about it, but I got the distinct impression that they believed I was going to make a life with Carolyn. But I wouldn't let my mind go there. *Yet.* I was still a struggling model, and I had a long way to go before I would be able to support a family.

My friends also assumed that this was it; that I'd found my missing half. If I showed up without her, they were disappointed. They loved taking her clubbing in New Haven. I remember one night they were ribbing her about being too perfect, and they kept looking for something about her—anything at all—that fell short of perfection.

Then my friend Tommy noticed her feet. They were pretty big feet for a woman. Not too big, given Carolyn's height, but if you looked at them—well, they were definitely *there.*

"Will you look at those flippers!" he said. Everybody laughed. From that day on, that was Carolyn's nickname: Flipper. I think she liked it, and I'm pretty sure she liked Tommy too. He was the best-looking one in the group, and she enjoyed flirting with him. Tommy ate it up, and in moments of weakness I actually found myself getting a little jealous.

On another visit home we found ourselves inside a pet shop, staring through the glass cage at a miniature pinscher puppy. We both fell in love with it. The owner said we could take it home for twenty-four hours, and if it didn't work out we could bring it back for a full refund. We took it home, to my parents' house, and it slept between us on the bed that night. In the morning, we took it out front and played with it, and we were more in love with it than ever. But suddenly Carolyn announced that she couldn't do it. There was genuine fear in her eyes. She said it was too much work, too big of a responsibility, too much of a commitment. (There was that word again: "commitment.")

"I can't even take care of myself," she blurted out. "How am I going to take care of a helpless little puppy?"

We took the little dog back and got our full refund, and, for an hour or two, we wandered around in a daze, neither of us able to utter a word. I guess we were both pretty choked up.

On our way back to the city from yet another weekend home, I asked Carolyn about the underwear campaign. There hadn't been any news in a while, and I figured I was out of the running. She was usually on top of these things, but often too busy to get involved in the early stages. Her job was to put the publicity machine into high gear when the time came, and the time still hadn't come—CK was still frantically looking for the right guy. Carolyn inquired on my behalf and discovered that my agency hadn't been lying to me after all: I really *was* in the running—along with about fifty other guys.

This went on for weeks and months. Click would report in from time to time to reassure me that I was still a candidate. I was pleased, but I wasn't going to get carried away: I knew my chances were slim to none.

But one night in September, Carolyn came over to the apartment, and I could tell she had something up her sleeve. She had a sly look in her eyes.

"What's up?" I said.

"Meow," she said, toying with me.

"Come on," I said. "What do you know that I don't know?"

She laughed. "They're down to six guys," she said. "And you're one of them."

"I wish you hadn't told me that," I said. I meant it too. I didn't want to get my hopes up.

"You don't get it, do you?" she said. "No matter what happens, you're on your way. You're making it as a model."

She had a point. I wasn't going to argue with that. We celebrated in bed. I was happy. She was happy. Life was good.

★   ★   ★

.A few weeks later—this was October 1993—she called and asked me to come over to her apartment. It sounded urgent, but she wouldn't say anything on the phone.

I hurried over. She was sitting on the edge of the bed. She looked pale and drawn.

"What's wrong?" I asked. With typical self-absorption, I thought this was about me. I thought it was bad news about the CK campaign.

"You're not going to like this," she said. "I'm pregnant."

Jesus. I sat down on the bed next to her. I didn't know what to say or where to look. "What do you want to do?" I asked.

"I don't know," she said. She had no energy at all; her voice was barely audible.

I took her hand in mine. "I'll do anything you want," I said. "We're going to be fine. I love you, and I've never been happier in my life."

"I can't have a child," she said, fighting tears. "I can't even consider having a child. It has nothing to do with you. I'm just not ready."

"Carolyn—"

She put a finger to my lips, shushing me. "I don't want to discuss it," she said gently. "This isn't your decision. I just need you to help me through this."

"I'll do whatever you want me to do," I said.

I spent the night. We held each other but didn't make love. The next morning she hurried off to work. She called me twice during the day—"Just to hear your voice"—and we spent the next two nights together—just holding on to each other, as if for dear life.

Friday morning she got up and dressed hurriedly, and we hustled over to the subway station. She was late for work again.

"You're still coming to Naugatuck, right?" I asked just before she hurried off. I couldn't help myself. I had to know. We were supposed to leave at the end of the day to hook up with my friends, *our* friends actually, for dinner and drinks, then hang with my family the rest of the weekend. I felt it was important to be around family, especially at a time like this. Not that we were going to share this difficult news with them, but having them near would be nice.

"Yes," she said, then added, "I'll talk to you later."

When she called, she said she didn't feel like going, but that I should go on ahead—my friends were expecting me. "I might come up tomorrow," she added.

I didn't like the "might." I didn't like the idea of leaving her behind. But she insisted. "I'll be fine," she said.

I took the train, hooked up with my friends, and we hit the bars in and around New Haven, but I didn't have much fun.

The next morning, slightly hungover, I reached her at home. She said she was sorry, but she was going to stay in town. She had plenty to do. I offered to come back on the next train, but she didn't want me to. "Please don't worry," she said. "I'm fine. Stick to the plan. I'll see you tomorrow."

"But I want to be with *you*," I said, but she wouldn't listen.

"I don't want your family to see me like this," she said.

I called her several times that day and well into the night, but I didn't get through, and she didn't return my calls. I tried not to worry, telling myself that she had probably turned off the phone and gone to bed early.

As soon as I got back to the city on Sunday, I went over and spent the night with her. We didn't make love again. This was the longest we'd gone without making love since getting back together. But I held her, and it was enough.

Monday morning, I walked her to the subway. On the way home, I passed a newsstand and saw something that stopped me dead in my tracks: a picture of her and JFK Jr. on the cover of the *New York Post*. They were sitting on a curb together, close, watching the

New York City Marathon. I called her at work and asked if she'd seen the paper.

"Yes," she said. "It's nothing."

"Nothing!" I was steamed. This was the weekend she was supposed to have been with me and my family, up in Naugatuck, and somehow she had managed to pull herself out of her depression to go for a little stroll with her friend John Jr. I was about to rip into her and she knew it, so she stopped me and told me she couldn't talk right then, but that she'd explain everything to me later.

We met at her place that evening. She reiterated that it was nothing. John Jr. had called and she'd been home alone, moping, so she decided that the fresh air might do her some good.

"Oh, really?" I said, and then my usually reliable impulse control failed me. "What about that copy of *People* magazine?"

I don't know why I said it. I just blurted it out. And it was too late to take it back.

"What copy of *People* magazine?" she asked.

"Don't act so innocent," I said. "The one you've got stashed under the kitchen sink."

"So you're going through my things when I'm not here?"

"No," I said. "I was looking for coffee filters."

"This is ridiculous!" she snapped. "Why are we even talking about this?! I told you already: he doesn't mean anything to me. He happened to call me and I was here and I went. That's it."

Now I remembered that I'd been unable to get through to her on Saturday night. I wondered if perhaps she hadn't been home; if perhaps she'd been with John. That seemed like the obvious answer, but when you're in love, there are certain things you don't want to see. And I certainly didn't want to see that. I wanted to ask her straight out, but I was scared. It seemed so ugly. And if it was true, where did that leave me?

"Why didn't you at least tell me that he'd called?" I said. "Why didn't you tell me you'd gone out with him? Why do I have to see in the paper a picture of my girlfriend sitting on the curb with JFK Jr. watching the goddamn marathon?"

"Michael, God—how many times do I have to tell you? He's just a friend. We just chatted. I think he's seeing Daryl Hannah."

Okay. Good. That worked. It gave me hope. I'd heard the rumor too.

It's not as if that was the only thing on our minds: we still had the pregnancy to deal with. Carolyn made an appointment. When the day came, I went with her, and it was even more horrible than I'd imagined. We got in a cab and held hands and said nothing all the way. It felt as if we were going to a funeral, which in a way we were. We got dropped off at a high-rise on the Upper East Side and took the elevator to the doctor's office. It looked like any other doctor's office: the small waiting room with the couch, the coffee table, the dog-eared magazines, and the framed prints on the walls. A nurse came out to get Carolyn and told me I had to wait there. I flipped through every magazine in the place, but I couldn't read a word. I couldn't even see the pictures. I kept thinking of Carolyn, what she must be going through, and how alone she must feel. I knew *I* felt alone. I wondered why I couldn't have gone in with her and held her hand.

After what seemed like days, but was really no more than an hour, the same nurse came out, smiled gently, and said I could go see Carolyn. She led me down the corridor and into a little room where Carolyn was lying on a cot, resting. I didn't say anything, just took her hand, and she held it tight. She had tears in her eyes, and they looked somehow dimmer, like she had less life in her. It scared me.

After a while, she felt strong enough to leave, and we took a cab back to her place. We didn't talk at all. I remember feeling horribly guilty. I thought we'd made a terrible mistake, that—young as we were—we should have had this child and tried to manage. I knew we could get by somehow, misgivings about my career notwithstanding. I loved Carolyn. I was afraid I was going to lose her over this. I felt terrible even thinking about that possibility and about the unborn child that we'd just lost—the child we'd *chosen* to lose. It wasn't a question of being pro- or antiabortion; it's just that it hits you in ways you never imagined possible.

Carolyn was devastated. She called in sick the next day and took the rest of the week off. With the exception of a few hours here and there, when I had to run off to a casting call or a shoot, I spent every minute at her side. But she refused to talk about it. I had to get her breakfast, lunch, and dinner. I had to make her get up so I could change the sheets. And still she wouldn't talk.

"Why don't you say something?" I asked after several days of near total silence.

"There's nothing to say," she said.

"You don't know. Just talking might help."

"Talking never helps," she said.

So I got nothing beyond a word here and there. I'm okay. I'm not hungry. Could I please get a glass of water? Where is the remote? When Sunday night rolled around, she simply pulled herself together. We went out and she had her first real meal in days. She'd mourned enough, it seemed, and it was time to move forward. Life throws some shit at you, and you deal with it. And she was dealing with it.

Something had changed though. I don't know what it was exactly. I felt less loved, and it gnawed away at me. Little things began to bother me, like the fact that we'd been going out for eight months and she still kept me hidden away. We went out with Gordon occasionally, and with Jules from time to time, but we never socialized as a couple with any other people. Not even people from Calvin

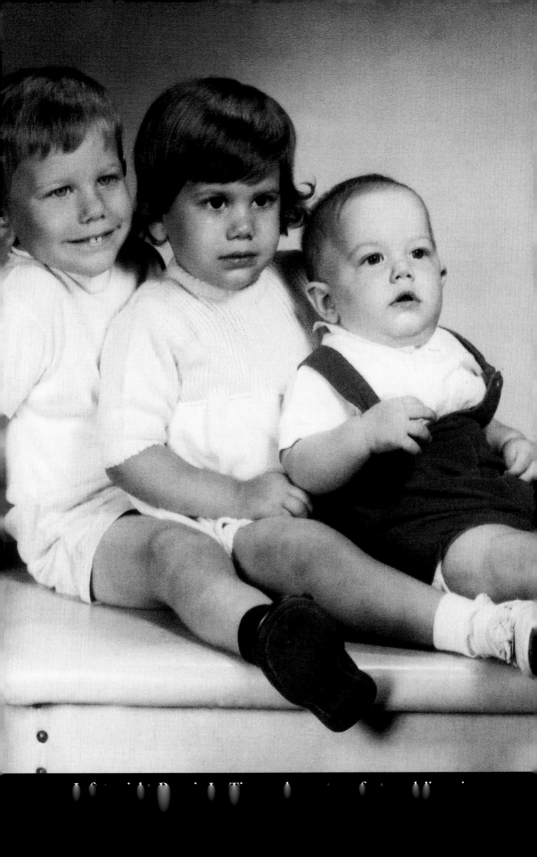

Ronnie Jr., me with baby Jessica, and Tina. The all-American family. BERGIN FAMILY

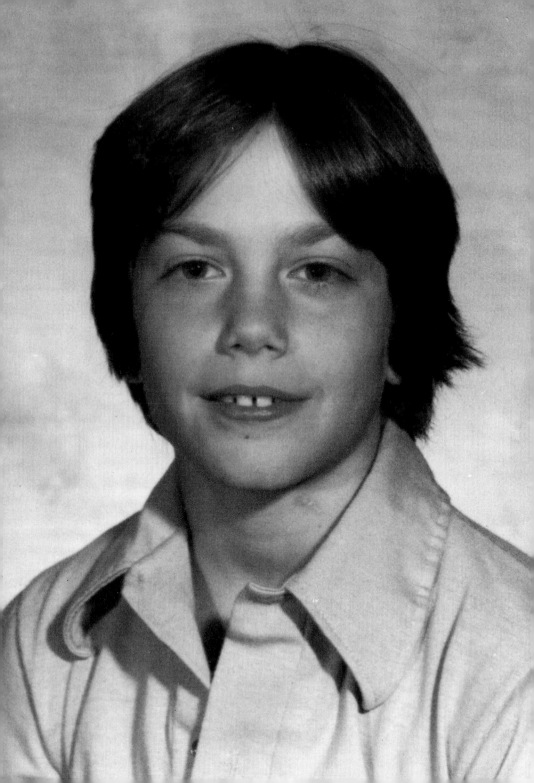

Captain of the Naugy High Hoopsters. Sports were my life.

Making a play at second base.

Graduation. That's me on the far left. I was a good student and proud of it.

A portrait of Carolyn as a school girl in 1983.
BOB LUCKY/CORBIS SYGMA

My senior class picture. To look at this, you'd never guess I had a future in modeling. BERGIN FAMILY

My Times Square debut, in April 1994, as the Calvin Klein Underwear Guy. BERGIN FAMILY

Posing naked for fitness photographer John Falocco. Photos from his shoot were used in several fitness magazines. JOHN FALOCCO

...with Carolyn on the stoop of my parents' home in Naugatuck. She's holding the miniature pinscher I bought for us. Sadly, we returned the puppy less than twenty-four hours later. BERGIN FAMILY

An intimate moment with Carolyn in the basement of our Atlanta home

Towering over Times Square in January 1995, during Part II of the CK campaign.

Four shots from my modeling career. MICHAEL TAMMARO

Mad About Him

Michael Bergin makes a move from Calvin Klein model to small-screen heartthrob and sets out to cultivate a career that is more than just a brief brush with fame

Carolyn looking beautiful, as always, in a sun dress.
As far as I was concerned, she couldn't take a bad picture.

Michael Bergin

Ironically, this poster was launched two days after Carolyn's
secret wedding to John F. Kennedy Jr. BERGIN FAMILY

Editorial gig for *Esquire* magazine shot by Troy Word. I guess leather was "in" back then. TROY WORD

John F. Kennedy Jr. and Carolyn taking a walk in the rain with
their dog, Friday. Both were very photogenic, as you can see.

John and Carolyn in New York City, October 1996.

The St. Christopher necklace Carolyn gave me for protection. She scratched the X and O on the back for "hugs" and "kisses."
BERGIN FAMILY

These cuff links were a Father's Day gift from Carolyn. I didn't receive them until long after her death. BERGIN FAMILY

Carolyn and John at a Cartier reception in 1996. This is how I remember Carolyn: laughing, happy, and always the life of the party. STEPHANE CARDINALE/CORBIS SYGMA

John and Carolyn at the funeral of Michael Kennedy, John's cousin. AP PHOTO/MARK LENNIHAN

Carolyn trying to get away from the relentless paparazzi.

John and Carolyn in Milan. No matter where they went, they were hounded by the photographers. Carolyn never liked that kind of attention. C. MASTRULLO/GRAZIA NERI/CORBIS SYGMA

Here's me as *Baywatch* lifeguard Jack "J.D." Darius.

Me and Pamela Anderson taking a break during the filming of
Baywatch: Hawaiian Wedding. BERGIN FAMILY

With Joy and our son Jesse, on October 8, 1999, minutes after his birth. BERGIN FAMILY

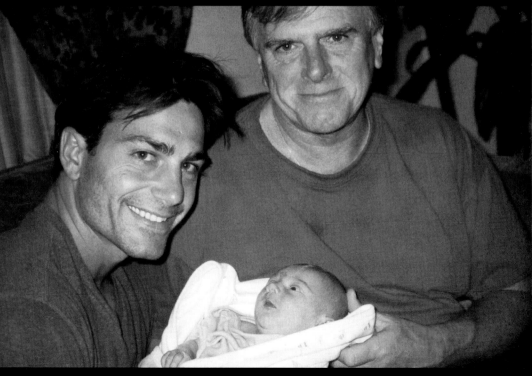

Three Bergin generations: my dad in L.A. visiting his first grandson. BERGIN FAMILY

Ever since my Calvin Klein underwear campaign, I've wanted to create and design my own underwear line. It's called "MB"— a.k.a. "Bergies." JOHN FALOCCO

Joy, Jesse, and me in Honolulu during the first season of
Baywatch Hawaii. BERGIN FAMILY

Here's my son Jesse, age 4, posing for the camera, trying to be like his Dad. BERGIN FAMILY

Klein, a few of whom I'd met in passing. And she still refused to define our relationship, still refused to acknowledge that we were together.

"Why can't you just look me in the eye and say I'm your boyfriend?" I asked her one cold night in a moment of weakness.

"I told you already," she said. "I don't like labels. And what difference does it make? You know I love you."

And I *did* know it. I guess. The way she looked at me. The way she clung to me. The way she made love to me. It all felt slightly diminished somehow, but it was still there.

So we went along, the two of us, and I forced myself to live without definitions.

Still, it bothered me. I'd be lying if I said otherwise. Why did she refuse to make the relationship public? Was there something wrong with me? Was I not good enough? Was it my age? Was I not classy enough?

And why was it I could never ask her any questions? Why was I letting her run the show? Why did I come crawling whenever she called? How had I allowed myself to accept that role? As always, I felt like the weaker half of the relationship, the weaker link; I felt the way a woman must feel when she's having an affair with a married man. But there was one big difference: I wasn't sitting around pining for her. We were always together. We were inseparable. And of course this only frustrated me further: Why couldn't she just come out and announce that we were a couple?

Her behavior fueled my insecurity. I wondered if in fact that's what she wanted—me to be insecure. An insecure partner is less likely to leave, and I knew she had abandonment issues. God! I had too much time on my hands—too much time to think and obsess. I needed a break—and I got it.

One afternoon the agency called. They had just heard that Calvin Klein was down to four or five guys, and I was one of them. Herb Ritts needed to test me and Calvin Klein had called Click about my availability.

Wow. Herb Ritts. Another world-class fashion photographer. I was incredibly nervous, even more so than usual. This didn't bode well at all.

In October, I made my way down to Industria Studios, trying not to hyperventilate. I kept telling myself over and over, *You are not nervous. You are not nervous. You are not nervous.*

Herb was in the middle of a shoot with some supermodel, so I waited. When they took a break, he came out and said hello, almost in passing. He was a short, thin guy, with Buddy Holly–style glasses, and he was very polite. "Come in, Michael. Relax. Everything's going to be fine."

He had one of his assistants set up the lights in another part of the studio, then went back to shoot his supermodel for another ten or fifteen minutes. That gave me more time to crumble. He returned, finally, and smiled at me. "Please take off your shirt," he said.

I took my shirt off and tried to relax as he began taking pictures. "Yes, Michael. Good, good. Relax."

Christ, what was wrong? Did I look that tense? I tried to calm myself. I told myself that they were down to five guys and that I was one of them, and how bad could I be? I mean, I was there with the great Herb Ritts, right?

I was in front of a white backdrop, one of those huge white rolls you see at all the photo studios, in nothing but my jeans. Herb was talking to me, cooing. "Turn this way. A little to the left. Smile. Good. Hold it. Flex the abs, Michael." And then, boom! Just like that, it was over. The whole thing hadn't lasted five minutes.

"Thank you very much for coming," he said and left.

I went home, knowing I'd fucked up and obsessing over it. *I was nervous. The camera must have picked that up. I totally sucked. He only shot two rolls. Obviously he knew I wasn't the guy.*

When I got back to the apartment, I told Mitch all about it. He listened and seemed fairly sympathetic, but there was an edge to the sympathy. He told me to stop worrying, that worrying wouldn't change anything, that I'd know soon enough.

It was strange. I'd been getting this weird vibe from Mitch lately. The truth is, I knew there was a part of Mitch that was kind of in love with me, but I didn't know what to do about it. I also knew he was jealous of Carolyn and our relationship. It was pretty solid now, and part of him must have hated that; he must have felt that it was ruining his (imaginary) chances with me.

Lately, when Carolyn left messages for me, Mitch would forget to tell me that she'd called. It was happening more and more often, and it was becoming something of an issue. Sometimes I'd get back to the apartment and he'd be on the phone with one of his male friends. He'd look up and say something coy, for my benefit. "I have to get off the phone now. My delicious boyfriend's back. And he gets upset if I don't give him my undivided attention." Then he'd hang up and smile at me, like he was my wife or something. It was a little weird, yes; but we kept it light. *I* did anyway. I couldn't imagine what was going on in his head, although I knew I'd never done anything to egg him on. Still, you know how it is with certain gay men: they never stop hoping. And Mitch was one of those men.

A few days later, I saw it more clearly. I came home after another night with Carolyn and found him sitting in the living room, looking drunk and disheveled. It was obvious he'd been up all night.

"Good morning, Michael," he said. He said it in a snippy way, and his words were slurred.

"What's happening?" I asked. "You okay?"

"Do I look okay?"

"No," I said. "Not really."

He began to cry. "Mitch?" I said. "What's wrong, buddy?"

And he blurted it out: "Do you have any idea how I've struggled to deal with my feelings for you?!"

I didn't answer. I was stunned. He bolted to his feet, ran to his bedroom in tears, and slammed the door. What was I supposed to do? I couldn't very well go into his room and try to comfort him? *I* was the problem. I decided to pretend it had never happened.

I called Click the next day to see if someone had heard anything from Calvin Klein. No one had. I called again at noon and again at the end of the day. Still nothing. "Michael," the booker told me. "Relax. We'll know when we know."

What the hell did she think I was? A Zen master? Relax, my ass!

The following week, the phone rang. Calvin wanted to see me in his office. For a fitting.

I'd met Calvin once or twice before, in passing, and when I arrived, he was waiting for me with several assistants.

"Hi, Michael," he said in that sweet way he has.

"Hi, Calvin," I said in that nervous way I have.

I tried on a few pairs of underwear. Wandered around. Tried on some jeans too.

Carolyn showed up. She came over and said hello in a very professional way, as if she really didn't know me all that well. It upset me a little, but there was nothing I could do about it. Then she left and Kelly Klein came in, all sweet and huggy. She was having a birthday party at Indochine that night, for sixty of her closest friends, and wondered if I'd come. This was a good sign. If I wasn't a serious candidate for the campaign, why had she invited me?

I tried to get in touch with Carolyn to let her know I was going to the party, but I was unable to reach her, and she was of course surprised to see me there. I walked over and got a perfunctory peck on the cheek—*Ho hum. Just another male model who wants to be my best friend*—and realized that there weren't going to be any big pronouncements about us that evening. Not that it would have been appropriate anyway. This was Kelly's birthday party.

I found myself talking to a man I'll call Tad Small. He told me he was a manager.

"One of my friends is making a movie, *American Psycho*, and you'd be perfect for the lead," he said.

This was utterly ridiculous—I'd never acted in my life (I wouldn't call *Whispers in the Dark* a real acting gig)—but a little flattery never hurt anyone. So I hung out with Tad and let him tell me that I was the best-looking man he'd ever seen. Then it turned out that he wasn't really a manager at all—not officially anyway. But he knew a lot of people. He knew Bret Easton Ellis, for example, who had written the novel *American Psycho,* and he knew a lot of other "happening" people, as he put it. And he used his social connections to get things he wanted.

But I quickly grew tired of talking to him and began looking around for Carolyn again. And of course she was busy. She was chatting and doing her public relations thing, even at Kelly's birthday, because it was her job and that's what was expected of her. So I went over and said good-bye to her—she was going up to Greenwich that weekend—and I went back to my apartment.

The whole way home, I kept thinking about Carolyn and the way she controlled our relationship. I thought that perhaps this was what is meant by "unconditional love." Though it wasn't unconditional at all, was it? There were plenty of conditions, and she made them all.

Mitch was at the apartment, and I joined him on the couch. We hung out and drank beer well into the night. Sometime during the early hours, Mitch opened up to me as never before about my relationship with Carolyn and how deeply it bothered him. I couldn't deny that our friendship had deteriorated of late, and now I knew why. Mitch went to bed a little while later, and I passed out around dawn thinking that it might be time to find my own place.

When I woke up, it was early afternoon, and Mitch was nowhere in sight.

I went out to the living room and saw that the phone was off the hook. I hung it up, then got a dial tone, and called Carolyn in Greenwich. "Hey," I said. "I miss you."

"If you miss me so much, why didn't you call me back?" she said.

"You called?"

"Yes," she said. "At eight this morning. To invite you up. Mitch answered and the phone went dead, and when I called back the line was busy."

Not cool.

Carolyn came back that night. I told her about my conversation with Mitch and his feelings for me.

"Michael," she said, and she took both my hands in hers. "Mitch is a great guy, and he's always been a friend to you. He's just in love with you and jealous of us."

She said that Mitch must have simply flipped out when she called early that morning, that hearing her voice after a sleepless night must have sent him over the edge, and that he was probably kicking himself for it now. But he'd get over it.

"Maybe," I said. "But I need to find an apartment of my own."

"You probably do," she agreed.

We fell asleep in each other's arms, but we didn't make love.

On Monday in early December, I got the call: an early Christmas present. "You're it, pal. You're the new Calvin Klein underwear guy."

I was stunned. I couldn't believe it. I called Carolyn at work. "Did you hear?" I asked.

"I only found out this morning," she said.

"You could have called," I said.

"No," she said. "I couldn't have."

And she was right. It would have been unprofessional.

"I'm in shock," I said. And when I got off the phone, I began to panic.

Shit. What if I'm not good enough? What if I can't pull it off?

I was absolutely fucking terrified.

4.

The Underwear Guy

Love reckons hours for months, and days for years
And every little absence is an age.
—John Dryden, *Amphitryon*

Carolyn took me out to celebrate the good news, and when we got back I called my parents to tell them all about it.

"Mom," I said. "I'm it. I'm the next Calvin Klein underwear guy!"

"That's nice, sweetie."

"No, you don't get it. This is huge! This is as prestigious as it gets."

"I'm very happy for you, honey," she said, her voice flat. It just wasn't registering. "I'm looking forward to Christmas," she said.

I was so wired, I hardly slept that night. The next morning the agency called and said there had been a change of plans. My heart sank. *I didn't get the job,* I thought. *It was all a big mistake.*

But fortunately, the change had nothing to do with me. The agency had opted to use Wayne Maser instead of Herb Ritts. I didn't know Wayne, but I'd heard that he was unfriendly and unpredictable. Suddenly Bruce Weber sounded just fine by me—Chinese relaxation techniques and all.

The next day there was an item about the campaign in the *New York Post*. Carolyn called me from the office to tell me about it.

"Michael Bergin, a relative unknown, is the new Calvin Klein underwear model." The blurb made it sound as if I'd beaten out thousands of hopefuls, including Brad Pitt, Woody Harrelson, and Anthony Kiedis. I wondered how newspapers managed to survive; they seemed to subsist on half truths and embellishments.

"Aren't you excited?" Carolyn asked me.

"If I wasn't so nervous, I'd probably be excited," I replied.

On the big day, in early December, I made my way down to Industria Studios, located, appropriately enough, in the heart of Manhattan's meat-packing district. I was told it was going to be a two-day shoot. My fee was $2,500 a day.

Kate Moss was already there, surrounded by hair and makeup people. I took the chair next to her and held up an eight-by-ten print I'd brought along to break the ice. It was from the Bloomingdale's shoot we'd done together several months earlier. I was in my jeans, with the edge of my underwear showing, and Kate was holding my hand, looking appealingly grungy. "Remember me?" I said.

"I remember," she said, smiling.

But before she could say anything else, one of the fitters came out to tell us that Maser was ready for me, that he'd get to Kate later. I was nervous and didn't want to go first, but I had no choice.

I went in and met a cold and very businesslike Wayne Maser. He grunted in my general direction and motioned toward the set. I went and stood against the white backdrop—that giant roll again—in nothing but my black briefs. I kept telling myself that I was going to kick ass, that I was feeling *good*. And I believed it.

One of the assistants was fiddling with the lights, and Maser took a look through the lens of his camera. Suddenly, he stood up looking angry and disgusted.

"Get this guy a beer!" he said to no one in particular.

"Excuse me?" I said.

"You're pretty tense, aren't you?" he said.

"Me?" I said. I was genuinely shocked. I'd been feeling solid, for a moment anyway.

"Yeah," he said disdainfully. *"You."*

I didn't know what to do. Maybe somebody at Click had told him that I had a tendency to get nervous, but I thought I'd been hiding it pretty well. A moment later one of the assistants showed up carrying a half dozen bottles of chilled beer and two shots of tequila. Fuck it. I started with a shot of tequila and chased it down with the first of several beers.

Not surprisingly, the morning went by in a blur. Endless posing, with plenty of brief pauses for refreshment. Maser never loosened up. When we broke for lunch, I passed out on a couch until someone woke me late in the afternoon to say that they were done with Kate. It was my turn again. I was feeling pretty groggy, but I suffered through another hour or two of solo shots and went home.

When I got back to my place, the phone was ringing. "It went great!" Carolyn said.

"Really?" I said. "How do you know? I don't remember much beyond my third beer."

As it turned out, Carolyn had been calling throughout the day to check up on me. I guess she was nervous on my behalf. She said I'd done fine, and that I should stop worrying and get to sleep. "You have another long day ahead of you," she said. "I'm sure that will go great too."

When I got to the set the next morning, I immediately asked for two shots of tequila, and I drank them there and then. "Breakfast," I said.

The shoot got under way. It was the two of us now, Kate and me, and it was all about heat and passion and sex. Maser kept pushing for more heat and more passion. It felt like he wanted borderline porn. At one point, I was on all fours, with Kate on my back, and Maser told me to turn my head as far as I could and kiss her.

Kate was very uncomfortable with this. She had a boyfriend at the time, Mario Sorrenti, a photographer who had shot her for those very effective Calvin Klein Obsession ads down in the Caribbean, where she had been made to look as if she were on drugs. She was very serious about their relationship and didn't feel like getting kinky with me. I understood, but Maser kept pushing. So I had a few beers and we met him halfway and got through it.

"Mario's very jealous," she told me. "He's not going to like this."

I wanted to tell her that Carolyn was very jealous too, and that she wouldn't like it much herself. But Carolyn wasn't jealous at all, and she wasn't even my girlfriend—in name anyway.

I didn't get any feedback about the shoot from anyone except Carolyn, and all she could tell me was that she'd heard it went beautifully. Two days later, she got a chance to sneak a look at the images, and she called to tell me that she was bowled over. "You look great!" she said.

An hour later, Click called. "You'll be going to Milan in January," an agent told me. "It's going to be marvelous."

"Milan? Marvelous?"

"Yes. You're going to be huge when this hits. You need to go to Europe now and start showing your pretty face."

"What about the pictures Maser took?"

"Don't worry. They're probably fine."

I didn't want to go to Milan. I didn't want to leave Carolyn. She didn't want me to leave either. We were already beginning to suffer from separation anxiety, and I hadn't even gotten my passport yet. On the way to the post office to fill out the application—I hadn't even known that you could get a passport through the postal service—I began to feel physically ill. I didn't want to get on a plane and fly across the Atlantic. Moving to New York had been hard enough for me.

I was at Carolyn's that night. "I have to get out of town," she said.

"You want to go up to my parents' this weekend?"

"No," she said. "I mean really out of town. I need a vacation. I think I'll go to Florida. Maybe I'll ask Jules to come with me."

My insecurity kicked into high gear. Why wouldn't she want to go with me? Was she still upset about the pregnancy? Was she blaming me? Then again, maybe this had nothing to do with the pregnancy, or with Jules, for that matter. Maybe this was about another man. Maybe this was about John Jr. Maybe he was waiting for her in Florida.

"Why don't you ask me to go?" I said.

"Would you want to go?" she asked. There was something off in her eyes. Something evasive. I'd never seen her like this. I felt like she was slipping away somehow.

"Of course I would," I said.

"How would I know that?" she asked.

"How would you know that?" I said, and I was steamed. "How would you know? Because I'm your boyfriend, that's how!" There. I'd said it. I'd put it out there. But I didn't honestly know what to expect. Maybe I half expected her to confirm it, to look me in the eye and tell me that I was right, that I *was* her boyfriend. It didn't happen though. She was looking at me strangely, and I was trying not to get worked up. If it wasn't another man—if it was just my own paranoia—maybe it was something else. Maybe she was just distancing herself from me because I was leaving for Milan and she couldn't handle it. Maybe she knew I was going to get big in this business, and she was worried about losing me. Then again, maybe I was crazy. Maybe I was overanalyzing this whole thing.

"Okay," she said. "Let's go together."

She could have said it with more enthusiasm, but I didn't complain. We decided to fly to Florida right after Christmas and celebrate New Year's together. Just the two of us: me and my sort-of girlfriend.

Then the holidays were upon us. I was going up to see my family, and she was off to see hers. A few days before Christmas, however, she surprised the hell out of me.

"I want you to come to Greenwich to meet the rest of my family," she said. I had met her mother briefly in New York on two occasions, in my capacity as Carolyn's *friend,* though her mother knew we were involved. But that was as close as I'd ever gotten to any of her family.

"You do?"

"Yes," she said.

I didn't know where that had come from, but I wasn't going to question it.

On Christmas Eve, I had an early dinner with my family as planned, then drove over to Greenwich. I was nervous. It meant a lot to me that she wanted me there. Her family had a nice house with a big yard in a pretty ritzy neighborhood. Carolyn came to get me at the door and introduced me to everyone. Her mother, Ann; her stepfather, Richard; her sisters, Lauren and Lisa; and some friends and relatives. She was very affectionate and kept her hand on my arm the whole time, which put me at ease. I couldn't help but wonder why she never acted this way in New York.

I'd seen pictures of houses like hers in architectural magazines. It was nicely furnished, with art on the walls and knickknacks that looked expensive. Everything was spotless and in its assigned place, and everyone—family, friends, guests—seemed to know his or her place too. They all seemed so comfortable. On the other hand, I was so worried about doing or saying the wrong thing that it made me even more quiet and shy than usual. Still, the family seemed to like me—or they acted like it anyway. They all went out of their way to make me feel at home. I tried to relax, but I kept thinking about the fact that I was there, and what it meant, and whether Carolyn often brought men home to meet her family.

We stayed until pretty late. Then the evening drew to a close and all the friends and relatives left, and it was just Carolyn, me, and the immediate family. They made me feel as if I was part of it, and I got the impression that they were rooting for us as a couple.

Then Carolyn asked me to spend the night in the guest room above the garage. Who was I to complain? She walked me over to the room, which was warm and cozy.

"I have a present for you," I told Carolyn.

"I have one for you," she said.

I gave her a stainless steel limited edition Olympus camera that she'd had her eye on for a while. She gave me a beautiful Swiss Army watch. We were like a couple of happy kids, alone in that cozy room.

"Meow," she said, and she curled up against me on the bed.

"Meow," I said back.

I left early the next morning, spent Christmas Day with my family, and the following day met her in Manhattan to pack for Florida. We left the next morning for the Pelican Cove Resort in a place called Islamorada, in the Florida Keys. We flew to Miami and drove the rest of the way.

The resort was beautiful and right on the beach. It was our first vacation together, and I was hopeful. But Carolyn was in a funk. She didn't want to leave the room, and, as usual, I couldn't get her to talk about it. "I'm all right," she'd say. "Don't worry. I'll be fine. It's nothing."

The first couple of days, I went out on my own from time to time, to take a dip in the pool, hustle up a game of volleyball, or go for a jog along the beach. I always came back to the room hoping she'd have snapped out of it, that she would be somehow transformed. But she stayed lost inside herself.

"This is wonderful," she said one evening. "I love being on vacation with you."

I'd never seen her look sadder.

On the third day, she left the room on her own and came down to the beach and saw me playing volleyball with some of the other guests. I began clowning for her. I'd jump real high and spike the ball with all my might, trying to get a laugh. She barely managed a smile, and the sadness wouldn't leave her face. I joined her and urged her to come for a walk, but she just wanted to go back to the room. She wanted to be held, so I hugged her and ordered room service. She didn't want anything. Not even mashed potatoes.

The next day I dragged her out and took some pictures of her with the new camera. I had somebody take a few shots of us by the pool and at the beach. She smiled and actually managed to look like she was having a good time. I thought, *Even when she's sad, she's the most beautiful woman I've ever seen.*

For the next few days, we ordered room service a lot. She'd watch TV and tell me to go out and enjoy myself, that it was fine, that this is what she needed. One night after we made love, she cried. I didn't know what to do. If there was ever a time to open up and talk, this was it. But Carolyn didn't talk. I honestly believe that she didn't know what was wrong. Maybe it was just life, different forces wearing on her.

On New Year's Eve I ordered strawberries with cream and a bottle of champagne, and we got into the Jacuzzi. She had a couple of strawberries and a sip or two of champagne, but she was tired, so we went back to the room. She fell asleep by ten. I went back out and had a few drinks with some people I'd met on the volleyball court. Shortly before midnight I returned to the room, woke Carolyn up, and told her it was almost time. I sat on the bed next to her and turned on the TV to watch Dick Clark do his annual countdown in Times Square. She made me turn it off.

"I hate Dick Clark," she said groggily. So I took off my clothes, got into bed next to her, and held her. And that was the New Year; that was our vacation. But I wasn't complaining. She was my girl, right? Through good times and bad.

Unfortunately, the minute we got back to New York, Carolyn's behavior took another odd turn. She refused to leave my side. If I went to the dry cleaner's, she went with me. If I had to stop at a newsstand for a paper, she'd be standing next to me, her body pressed against mine, holding on as if for dear life. If we were out at dinner, I couldn't reach for my wallet because she refused to let go of my arm. Now she was being affectionate in public—though of course only in places where we didn't risk running into people she knew—but I found it all a little unnerving. She'd pinch at my skin. Pinch pinch pinch. It had once been an endearing habit; now it had this frenetic quality to it. She was pinching me so hard that I had to keep switching sides. "Work on this arm for a while," I joked, but she didn't see the humor in it. And neither did I, I guess.

I didn't know what to do. I'd seen that kind of clinginess before—in *children*. On some level it was flattering, but I also knew it was unhealthy; I knew something was very wrong.

I kept trying to find out what was troubling her, but in typical Carolyn fashion she kept her thoughts and feelings to herself. Again, it was nothing; she was fine; life was wonderful. But as I look back on it now, I suspect I know what it was. Carolyn wasn't much good at being alone, and I think she was anticipating a great deal of loneliness. I'd be leaving for Milan soon, and I'd be gone for three weeks. She couldn't bring herself to call me her boyfriend, but she already knew she was going to miss me. Those three weeks seemed like an eternity to both of us.

"Meow," she said one night, sounding forlorn.

"I miss you already too," I said.

Later, I woke up and found her bawling in the tiny bathroom, trying to muffle her sobs. I brought her back to bed and made love to her, but as soon as we were done she was crying again.

The next morning she was up and dressed in seven minutes flat, and off to work. She called me a dozen times during the day, just to say hello, and called me just as she was leaving work, so that I would be waiting for her at her place as soon as she walked in. I remember she was a little late coming back that evening, because she had stopped to pick up the pictures we'd shot at Islamorada. She had insisted on taking the film in herself, but when she arrived with the pictures half of them were missing.

"What happened to the shots of you and me?" I said. "There's only me in here."

"I tossed them," she said. "I looked hideous. And most of them didn't turn out very well anyway."

That was patently untrue. Carolyn couldn't look terrible if she tried. She had been seriously depressed in Florida, but she still looked very beautiful.

Then a horrible thought occurred to me: What if Carolyn was protecting herself? Maybe she didn't want any record of our relationship. Maybe she was thinking about the future, and maybe that future had nothing to do with us. It was an ugly thought, and I'm not proud of it, but I'm not sure I was too far off the mark. In New York, I felt like her "mistress," hidden away. *Sure, we'll go on a fabulous trip to the Côte d'Azur, honey, but no one can know about it.*

The next morning, a Saturday, she leapt out of bed—a woman transformed. "I'm taking you shopping," she said. She was wired and excited. The depression had lifted. Whatever had been bothering her was gone. Overnight, she'd become another person. That day and the ones that followed became all about me and my trip. She was going to prepare me for Milan, physically, psychologically, and emotionally. Carolyn was a woman on a mission. She made me buy shirts, jeans, sweaters, and had me splurge on a huge, black military-style duffel bag because it was *cool*. She made me get a haircut and bought me shampoo, new nail clippers, and a hairbrush. The hairbrush was fine, but she knew I'd never use the nail clippers: I'd been biting my nails since I was four.

I spent Friday and Saturday at her place, watching movies, ordering in, making love. We had never made love so slowly in our lives—or with such tenderness. She kept toying with me, interrupting me. I guess she didn't want it to end.

Before we knew it, however, it was Sunday, and time for me to go. She had been full of nervous energy since morning, and she was still wired, smiling a little too fiercely. You know what I mean—the smile didn't seem to correspond to her true feelings. Me? I wasn't smiling. I was miserable. Three weeks without Carolyn! How was I going to get through it?

We went downstairs and hailed a cab, and I put my huge duffel bag into the trunk. It was so big it almost didn't fit. We laughed about it, but suddenly we were standing on the sidewalk, next to the waiting cab, facing each other, and we had to say good-bye. Her eyes filled with tears. They flooded out of her, a regular torrent.

"Oh, God," she moaned. "You forgot the hairbrush."

It wasn't about the hairbrush.

"I don't want to go either," I said.

"I know," she said, trying to be strong. "But it's not as if you have a choice. And three weeks will go by fast, right?"

"No," I said.

She reached into her pocket and handed me two small wrapped packages. "I love you," she said. "You know that, right?"

I couldn't respond. I almost lost it right there.

"Call me," she said.

I got into the cab, and she closed the door but signaled for me to roll down the window. She reached through the open window and held my arm so tightly I thought her fingernails would draw blood.

"Meow," she said, and suddenly she was crying again. I didn't meow back. I couldn't find it in me. Then she turned toward the driver and told him to go. As he pulled away, I turned in my seat and watched her, but she was already hurrying off, her back to me.

"Love!" the cabdriver said, grinning. "It's really something, eh?"

Yeah. Something.

I didn't feel like talking. I turned my attention to the two packages in my lap, and tore the wrapping off one. It was an English-Italian dictionary. The other was a cassette of sappy love songs that one of Carolyn's girlfriends had made for her. She said she hated it, but I think she secretly liked it. She liked to pretend she was tougher than that. Well, I wasn't quite as tough, and I was glad to have it.

The flight from New York to Milan felt like the longest flight of my life, which in fact it was. I hated every minute of it. I missed Carolyn, my family, my bed.

The wet, cold, and snowy weather in Milan matched my dark mood. I handed a cabdriver a slip with the directions to my hotel. I expected it to be in the heart of the city, but it was a half an hour out of town. The agency had put me up in a cheap *pensione,* far from the action, along with two other models, since it was all we could afford. That only depressed me further.

I didn't even have time to settle in. I said hello to the guys and hit the ground running: my first appointment, with Click's Italian counterpart, was in less than forty-five minutes, so I headed right back into town. I bought a subway map and found my way over, and I didn't exactly feel welcome. Everything was rush rush rush. And in Italian. So I understood nothing in a hurry.

I wasn't there long. They gave me an address, pointed out the location on my subway map, and sent me on my way to a casting call.

It was Fashion Week in Milan, but it wasn't anywhere near as glamorous as it sounds. It never stopped raining. I was cold and wet and eternally lost. I'd leave the *pensione* by seven A.M. and wouldn't get back until ten. In between, I shuffled from one cattle call to the next, hopping into buses, subway cars, and the occasional taxi (when I was running late). I was so stressed about finding my way to the right place at the right time that I never ate. I lost ten pounds in the space of a week. I looked gaunt, almost haunted. Who'd hire me now? Then again, maybe I could go for the gaunt, haunted, druggie look; it had worked for some.

But I somehow managed to book runway shows, starting with Armani. No one knew who I was yet—the Calvin Klein shoot was over, but the campaign was still several months away—and they treated me accordingly: like a complete nobody.

Then Valentino sent for me. He said he was doing a special show in Florence the following week and wanted me to be a part of it. He was on the short side, and pleasant looking, with an easy smile and a bad-boy gleam in his eye. Apparently he had heard good things about the underwear campaign, and he couldn't have been kinder.

"I hear nice things about you," he said in his thick accent. "Very, very nice."

That night, back at the *pensione,* just as I was drifting off to sleep, exhausted, someone knocked on the door and said there was a call for me in the lobby. I groped my way downstairs and picked up the receiver.

It was Gordon Henderson, and he proceeded to rip me a new asshole. I'd been gone more than a week and I hadn't even bothered calling Carolyn. I apologized but still managed to come up with a series of excuses: I was busy. It was cold. I was sick and couldn't even eat. I was too depressed to think. Plus, the nearest international telephone was half a mile away, and you needed a phone card to use it.

"That's lame," he said.

"I know," I said. "Is she pissed?"

"Hold on," he said.

"Hello?" It was Carolyn. I hadn't realized she was right there, with him.

"Hey, baby, how you doin'," I said. "I've missed you."

"How's Milan?" she asked very matter-of-factly. Almost cold, actually.

I told her it was hard and not much fun, then I apologized for not calling and said I missed her horribly.

"Then why haven't you called?" she said, and her voice cracked with emotion.

"I don't know, honey. I've missed you so much. I'm just trying to get through this as fast as I can."

"Well, good luck," Carolyn said tersely, and suddenly the call was over because she had to run. I wondered if she thought that I was having the time of my life—just traveling, partying, and meeting women. I wasn't of course, but I still felt like shit. I went back to my room and slept fitfully.

A few days later, I walked half a mile in the freezing rain to get to the phone and called her at home. She wasn't there, so I left a message on her machine. "I miss you. Only twelve more days. I love you."

Then it was time for the Valentino show, so I hurried off to catch the bus that was going to take me to Florence. It wasn't hard to find. There were two dozen male models waiting on the corner. When the bus finally arrived, we piled on. All of the guys were in visibly high spirits, laughing and horsing around, but not me. I took a seat in back and hoped no one would sit next to me.

It was a beautiful ride, but the beauty was lost on me. As the bus made its way through the mountains, I slipped on my headphones and listened to the tape Carolyn had given me for the tenth time. And I know this sounds corny, but there was one song on there by Michael Bolton that really got to me. It's called "Said I

Loved You . . . but I Lied." The title is misleading, but the lyrics really nail it:

> *"I said I loved you but I lied,*
> *'cause this is more than love I feel inside."*

It certainly was more than love, and Bolton had it right: Carolyn really *did* shine a light on my heart; she really *had* stepped out of my dreams and into my life; she really *was* a taste of heaven. It just killed me. I listened to the words over and over. I thought about the day I'd left New York, almost two weeks earlier. About the way Carolyn had held on to me through the window of the cab and the way she'd cried. I thought about how much I missed her, how lonely I was without her, and how badly I wanted to get home to her.

When we got to Florence, I managed to pull myself together, partly because I was too busy to think. There was a full day of fittings and rehearsals, time for a quick dinner, then it was back to the hotel to crash and get rested for the show.

There's really not all that much to a runway show, not for the models anyway. They arrive when they're told to arrive and wait backstage with everyone else. It's crowded with dressers, makeup artists, manicurists, publicists, personal assistants, even camera crews. As the time draws nearer, one can hear the crowd gathering outside, beginning to take their seats, and some of the key players tend to get hysterical.

But not most models. They just sit and wait until they're told to go on, then make their way down to the end of the runway, where people stare and ooh and aah. Then they turn around and go back, right through the curtains, into the arms of all these crazed people. Someone helps them change and someone else messes with their hair and a third person takes the shine off their forehead. Then they do it again. And maybe a third and a fourth time. In between, if they're good, and if there's time, they might even get a sandwich. Not very glamorous, is it?

All that hysteria, and my job as a model is to not let it faze me. My job is to get out there and do what I've been asked to do. And it's not as if there's room for a lot of spontaneity. Every single step, every turn, every nod of the head, every smile, every frown, every brooding look has all been perfectly choreographed. A model is an actor, and like an actor, expected to hit the marks.

It was a lot of work for very little money, and I was lucky if I covered the airfare and accommodations. But one has to do it for the exposure. That is the name of the game.

Valentino invited me to dinner at a local restaurant that evening, along with a select group of close friends and one or two other models. There was champagne, caviar, fine wine, and enough food for a small army. But I wasn't in a great mood. I was still pining for Carolyn. At one point, Valentino cornered me and asked me what was wrong. He was being very sweet, *too* sweet. He was basically flirting with me, but I made it clear, as gently as possible, that I wasn't interested. He smiled and said, "I can see from your eyes that you are thinking about a woman. Be careful she doesn't break your heart." He said it nicely, supportively, then went off to enjoy his other guests. I thought he handled himself with a lot of class. He didn't use his power to intimidate me. He was just a man who happened to be interested in other men, doing what he did. And if he'd been hurt by the rejection, he didn't let it show.

After another week of cattle calls, fittings, runway shows, and shoots, it was time to go home. I called Carolyn and left a message with my flight information. I didn't expect her to meet me at the airport, but I could hope, couldn't I?

She wasn't at the airport of course, so I took a cab back to the apartment on Twentieth Street and called her at work as soon as I came through the door. She wasn't there, so I left another message—"I'm home!"—and tried again later in the day. Still no answer, so I left one more: "Hey, honey. I'm here and I'm dying to see you."

Nothing. I didn't understand it. I'd been back since morning, I'd been calling all day, and as night fell I was still calling. And she *knew* I was back. Maybe she was still mad at me for not having called from Milan.

I phoned Gordon. He welcomed me home and tried to make small talk, but I just wanted to know about Carolyn. "I don't know where she is," he said. "She's missing in action."

I was fit to explode. I had been looking forward to this moment to the point of desperation, and she was nowhere to be found. I called again that night and her girlfriend Jules answered the phone. She didn't know where she was either, but she said she'd be sure to tell her that I'd called.

I still didn't hear back, so I kept calling. Dialing and redialing like a man possessed. Finally, as the sun was coming up, Carolyn answered the phone. "Hello?" she said groggily.

"Carolyn! Christ. It's me."

"What?" she said, her voice thick with sleep and anger. "What do you want? Why are you calling me at six in the morning?"

"What the fuck is going on?" I said. "I've been calling you all goddamn day and night. I've left messages everywhere!"

"Well I'm sorry I couldn't be there for you," she said, and there was a real edge to her voice. "I had a dinner to go to. I have a life too, you know. It's show season for us too."

"What a crock!" I said and hung up, enraged. A moment later I called back, but she didn't answer.

I reached her at work later in the morning and insisted on seeing her. She agreed to meet me for lunch, but she only did so to get me off the phone. We hooked up near her office and suddenly she didn't have time to eat. She only had a few minutes. I knew she was busy—it really *was* the middle of show season and the CK publicity machine was in high gear—but this was going too far.

"Is something wrong?" I asked. "Just tell me."

"Nothing's wrong," she said. "Can we not talk about this now? I'm really, really swamped."

So she went back to the office, and I went back to my apartment and slept like the dead. On Sunday night, I went over to her place. She opened the door and kissed me on the cheek as if I were a brother-in-law once removed. It was really crushing.

"That was great," I said.

"Please, Michael. Don't. I'm exhausted."

We sat down on the mattress. I didn't know what to say, so I told her what a lousy time I'd had in Milan and again apologized for having failed to call. She didn't say much, and I found myself trying to fill the silence with stories about some of the shows, about Florence, about losing my way in the subway, about all the crazy Italians. She nodded absently now and then, but she didn't seem to be listening.

"You're really pissed, aren't you?" I said, stating the obvious.

"What do you expect?" she said. "You go away for three weeks and you don't call and I worry myself sick."

Okay. We were making progress. I was getting it out of her. But I began to wish she'd *show* her anger. She seemed so sad and depleted: so *not* Carolyn.

That night, I made love to her and felt like I was alone in the room. She was absent, barely participating. I felt as if that trip to Milan had ruined everything, and that I'd come home to a changed woman. I felt hopeless. I lay there and listened to her steady breathing until I fell asleep.

She was up earlier than usual because she had a lot of work to do, and I got up and left with her. On the way out, I noticed a beautiful gray sweater—a man's sweater—by the foot of the bed. It was a mock turtleneck, with an unusually thick weave, and it struck me as being unlike any sweater I'd ever seen before.

I walked Carolyn to the subway and hurried back to my place to get ready for a fashion show for *Esquire* magazine. I had a busy week myself, and it was just getting under way. When I arrived for the show, a few minutes late, all the models were already standing next to their appointed racks. As I came through, I noticed one of the models, this guy I'll call Tyler, and I thought to myself that he was probably the best-looking man I had ever seen in my life. I'm not exaggerating. I am the straightest guy in the world, but I know when a guy is handsome, and Tyler was beyond handsome. He was chiseled and perfectly proportioned, and he had piercing blue eyes and long hair. The assistants kept walking past to get better looks at him, and these people are jaded—these are people who deal with beauty every day. Then, just as we were getting ready for the show, Tyler turned to look at me. He held the look for a moment, and my heart skipped a beat. And at that moment, I knew; I simply knew. Carolyn was fucking this guy.

I tried to tell myself that I was just being paranoid, but I was sure I was right. I couldn't shake the feeling. I called Carolyn right after the show. It was nuts. I wanted to ask her if she was fucking Tyler, but I managed to control myself. I even controlled myself when she said she couldn't see me that night. She was sorry; she was just too damn busy with work. Great! It's Monday, I'm barely back from Milan, and she can't see me. We'd been inseparable for months, now this? Christ. The coldness was killing me.

Tuesday morning, I did a brunch and a runway show at a local bistro for *GQ*. I was one of five models, and so was Tyler. He walked in wearing the beautiful gray sweater I'd seen at the foot of Carolyn's bed. I couldn't breathe. Jesus.

Okay. So maybe it's a coincidence, I thought, trying to calm myself down. It wasn't a one-of-a-kind sweater, right? Then again, it certainly could have been. Carolyn often got samples of Calvin Klein items that weren't in production and might never go into production. And there was something about that goddamn sweater that kept gnawing at me.

I asked one of the assistants about Tyler—up until that point all I knew was his first name—and she said, "Oh, isn't he gorgeous? He's doing the new Calvin Klein suit campaign." And right then I just goddamn knew. I was burning up inside. I had to say something, so I went up to Tyler and smiled.

"That's a great-looking sweater," I said. "Who makes it?"

Tyler said he didn't know. He went to look at the tag, but there wasn't one. The sweater was probably a Calvin Klein prototype. My heart sank.

"I guess I'm out of luck," I said, trying to keep the emotion out of my voice. "Where'd you get it?" He said it wasn't even his—a friend had lent it to him.

And that was it. That was the confirmation I needed. I walked off, looking for a phone. I felt like I was in the middle of a bad game of Clue. *The male model. With his dick. In her bedroom.*

I reached Carolyn at work and exploded: "I'm in this goddamn fucking bistro working with some fucking asshole model that you just happen to be fucking!" I was talking so fast that Carolyn couldn't understand me, so I had to repeat myself. She was floored. She told me I was crazy, that I didn't know what I was talking about.

"He's wearing your goddamn sweater," I shouted. "The one I saw in your apartment the other night."

Carolyn immediately came up with a great story; she was practically laughing. "Oh my God! You mean Tyler? That's Samantha's brother. You know my friend Samantha?!"

No, I didn't know her goddamn friend Samantha. I didn't know any of her friends except Jules and Gordon. But she went on and on about it: how Samantha borrowed the sweater from her and how

Samantha and Tyler lived together and how Tyler no doubt borrowed it from his sister.

"You're being paranoid," she said. "You have it all wrong. I only just met Tyler. He's doing our suit campaign."

Well, at least she admitted that much. So I decided to believe her.

I knew Carolyn had a thing about good-looking men, but I also knew that Carolyn didn't sleep around. Maybe I *was* being paranoid. Maybe it was all me.

"I'm sorry," I said. "I don't know what's wrong with me." I felt like the married guy who comes home and confronts his wife with evidence of adultery. If she denies it, he can accept it. But what if she looks him in the eye and says, "You know what, honey? You're right. I am cheating on you. This marriage is over." If my hunch was correct, I didn't want to know about it. I didn't want it to be over between us. Isn't that messed up? Even if Carolyn was lying, even if she was sleeping with Tyler, there was a part of me that preferred not to know. I really didn't want to lose her.

I got through the show without looking at Tyler and caught a shuttle to Boston for a half-day shoot at Filene's, a well-known department store. Then I caught an evening shuttle back and called Carolyn from the airport. She told me to come over. We went to sleep without making love. I had plenty of room on the bed that night. It didn't make me happy. I felt all emptied out and very confused.

I didn't see Carolyn the next day or the day after that. I saw her the following weekend, but she only had time for lunch. It felt like it was over, but we were in that strange place where neither of us was willing to acknowledge it. I certainly didn't want it to be over, but I didn't know about her. She seemed more resigned to it, more ready to move on.

The following week, on a cloudy February afternoon, still feeling very much adrift, and very low emotionally, I got a tip on a studio apartment on Eighth Street, near Sixth Avenue, in the heart of Greenwich Village. I went over to see it, met with the landlord, and charmed my way into it. My very first apartment, a place of my own.

I went back to Twentieth Street and told Mitch that I was moving out. Things had changed pretty dramatically between us since I had started dating Carolyn. Still, a part of me didn't want to leave. After all, Mitch had welcomed me into his home and his life. He had given me a head start in the modeling world by building up my portfolio and introducing me to key people. And he had always treated me well. I would miss him.

I called Carolyn to tell her I'd found a new place that was even closer to her place, and she was nice but distant. I kept thinking about Tyler and the gray sweater. I wondered whether he was there at that very moment.

I moved into my new place on a Tuesday morning. There was nothing to it. I had my red futon, my big duffel bag, a couple of suitcases, and it all fit into one cab. It was a lonely feeling, walking in there, looking at that small space and thinking, *This is your life, Michael Bergin*. I should have been positive about it—not all that long ago I'd been opening doors at the Paramount, struggling to make ends meet—but it was hard to feel good because I'd lost Carolyn.

One night I felt so unbearably alone that I went up to Joe's Café to see the old gang. I was hoping I'd run into Carolyn, but I didn't of course. She hadn't been there in months. Keith and Jason were both there, however, and so was this actress I'd met in passing many months earlier. The actress and I went back to my place and she didn't leave for seven days. It was a week of wild, angry sex. I didn't want her. I wanted Carolyn: my soul mate, my magical missing half. But so much for the goddamn fairy tale.

The following weekend, Tommy and some of my buddies came down from Connecticut to keep me company and try to lift my spirits. I called my actress friend, and we took the boys to a club to show them a good time, Manhattan-style. And wouldn't you know it? There was Carolyn. With Tyler. Not Tyler's illusory sister, just goddamn perfect-specimen Tyler, over in a corner, having drinks with my Carolyn. I felt like someone had just driven a knife into my gut. I almost threw up. At that moment, Carolyn turned and noticed me and the gang. She smiled and waved like it was the most natural thing in the world.

She came over, still smiling, all lit up and friendly. She knew the actress from Joe's Café, and she knew Tommy and most of the Connecticut contingent. She gave me a little kiss on the cheek, but I was tense and she sensed it. After some small talk with the others she said good-bye and went back to sit with Tyler. It was very awkward. My friends were there to help me forget her, and there she was, not twenty yards away, having a drink with another man and turning to look at me now and then. I got the impression that she wasn't too happy about seeing me with another woman.

"I can't do this," I told Tommy. "I'm leaving."

"Come on, Michael!" he said. "Sit down. Relax. You're with us."

But I couldn't do it. I was really messed up. I sort of wished that I could have found it in myself to be angry at Carolyn so that I could've drunk myself into a stupor. But how could I be angry at her? I was still nuts about her.

I didn't know what to do about her or about my bad feelings. I felt weighed down with sadness and frustration. I needed to be alone, so I told my actress friend that I was leaving, and that she should hang with Tommy and the boys. She wasn't happy about it, but I wasn't thinking about her happiness at the moment. All I was thinking about was my *un*happiness.

I turned to go and noticed Carolyn looking at me, her brows furrowed. She could see I was on my way out, and she hurried over and told me to please not leave; she wanted to talk to me. I watched as she rejoined Tyler for a moment. I couldn't hear what she was telling him, not at that distance, but it looked like she was being pretty matter-of-fact about it. Maybe *too* matter-of-fact. Then she joined me and we left together.

"You were going to leave without saying good-bye?" she said.

I couldn't believe she'd say something like that. Putting *me* on the defensive. I wanted to get mad. I wanted to take her by the shoulders and shake some sense into her. Did she have any idea how I felt about her? Did she have any idea how badly I was hurting?

"Carolyn, Christ," I began. "I just saw you with—"

"Please," she said, cutting me off. "Let's not go there. Tyler's just a friend."

A friend. Sure. Every man Carolyn had ever known was just a friend.

I felt like a wimp. "You expect me to believe that?" I asked.

"I *need* you to believe that," she said.

We went back to her place and made love. We instantly became aware of how much we'd missed each other. I missed the way she smelled, the way she touched me, the look in her eyes. In the throes of lovemaking, everything about us felt completely right.

I felt we were back, that it was just like it used to be. Only I was forced to admit to myself that it was a tiny bit different. We'd been with other people—well, *I* had anyway, and it certainly looked as if she had—but we didn't talk about it. Our reluctance to face facts was like a poison to both of us. There was tension there: mistrust, caution.

It went on like this for several months. On-again, off-again. There was plenty of heat, and there were plenty of cooling-off periods. It wasn't until that summer that I felt I could invite her up to Naugatuck again.

"I'm going up for the weekend," I said. "Friends of mine are having a big party. Wanna go?"

"You want me to go?"

"Sure," I said. "If I didn't, I wouldn't ask."

So she came. When we got to Naugatuck, I told her my ex-girlfriend Rachel was going to be at the party. I didn't think it was a big deal, but Carolyn was floored. She didn't want to go; she didn't want to meet Rachel. She knew how much Rachel had meant to me. Why was I putting her through this?

I'd never seen her like that. I kept telling her it wasn't a big deal. Rachel was in the distant past. In fact, she had recently met another guy and was leaving Naugatuck and moving across the country to be with him. This helped, but only marginally. Now Carolyn was worried about what she was going to wear. She hadn't brought anything she liked, so she asked if she could go through my sister's closet. She found a little something there and took a little something else from my mother's closet. Then she borrowed some makeup and transformed her face, but not in a good way.

"Honey," I said. "You don't even look like you."

"What?" she snapped. "You don't like the way I look?"

Wow. Loaded question. I said she looked fine, if a little different, but she didn't look fine at all. Instead of her usual seven minutes, Carolyn had spent two frenetic hours trying to put herself together, and the result was not pretty: she'd become another person—a lesser, more garish version of herself.

"No, no," I insisted. "I really like it. I don't mean 'different' in a bad way."

When we got to the party, Carolyn found a seat on one of the couches, parked herself in front of a bowl of chips, and helped herself to one handful after another. She saw Rachel and Rachel saw her, but Carolyn was giving off such an intensely hostile vibe that Rachel, wisely, decided not to come over.

"Is it time to leave yet?" Carolyn said. We hadn't been there ten minutes. And ten minutes later she asked again. You'd think I would have written the evening off as a fiasco, but the truth is that I'm a guy like any other, and in a typical-guy way, I sort of ate it up. I saw it as a measure of Carolyn's feelings for me. Her discomfort and jealousy told me she still loved me.

Here's a story you can file under *Plucked Eyebrows, Part II.*

We were at her place one Saturday morning, trying to find the energy to get up, go to the flea market, and pretend that our lives were back on track. I had a busy week ahead of me with Saks. I'd been doing a lot of work for the store in those days, at five thousand dollars a day, and had just been booked for a ten-page spread to exhibit the store's latest line of suits.

Carolyn reached over and straightened one of my eyebrows. "Don't you dare touch my eyebrows," I joked.

"I'm not thinking about your eyebrows," she said, smiling. "I'm looking at your hair. I think you should put some subtle highlights in your hair."

"You do?"

"Yes," she said. "Pass me the phone."

She called Brad Johns, her stylist, and asked him if he could squeeze me in somehow because I had a big shoot coming up. Of course he said yes—he would do anything to accommodate her.

I went over that afternoon. Brad was very effusive. He sat me down next to Carol Burnett and went to work, rushing between one client and another. When I got out of the chair, two hours later, I was a blond. It was pretty weird.

"Is this what Carolyn wanted?" I said.

"You look marvelous," Brad said.

Carolyn thought I looked marvelous too, or that's what she said anyway. But I got the feeling she thought it was a little much.

On Tuesday, I showed up for the shoot with photographer

Patrick Demarchelier, another fashion genius. The Saks rep was there as well, and when I walked through the door, his jaw practically hit the floor. "What happened to your hair?" he asked.

"You don't like it?" I asked.

The rep didn't answer. He went off to find a phone, called my agency, and then came back to get me, fuming. "They want to talk to you," he said. I got on the phone and the booker ripped me a second asshole. *Who the hell do you think you are, dying your hair blond?* When she was done with me, the fuming rep got back on the phone. More angry words were exchanged, but it soon became apparent that they couldn't afford to reschedule, so the shoot went ahead as planned, thank God—this was for ten grand.

I went back to Carolyn's at the end of the day and told her what had happened. I was pissed.

"Meow," she said.

"Don't fucking meow at me," I said. "I'm not screwing around here."

"Fine," she said. "What do you want me to say? I'm sorry."

In the old days, I would have laughed off this business with my hair. But I wasn't laughing now. And neither was she. This only depressed me further. It made me realize that our relationship was just limping along, with a good moment here and there. What the hell were we doing? Everything felt forced, unreal, unnatural. And we were always on edge lately, always on the verge of an argument.

The ad for Saks turned into a fiasco. The technicians tried to fix my hair color in the lab, but it didn't work out as planned. There were ten pages of me in suits, and I looked like I was wearing a helmet on every page. I wasn't happy, and I was sure Saks wasn't happy either.

At the end of March, after another up-and-down week with Carolyn, she called me from work one afternoon and said we needed to talk. I thought we were going to talk about the relationship, but when I got to her apartment I found out this was about something else altogether.

"I'm pregnant," she said.

This was seriously fucked up. I was totally thrown.

"Is it mine?" I said, my impulse control failing me again.

That was the wrong thing to say. Carolyn was livid. "How dare you ask me that?" she said. "I can't believe you still think I slept with Tyler!" She didn't say she *hadn't* slept with him of course, but she managed to put me on the defensive again. She couldn't believe that I had the temerity to accuse her of infidelity. She insisted that the baby could *only* be mine. And of course I believed her. When you're in love, you believe anything.

When the drama was over, when we were done with the ugly words and the recriminations, I told her I wanted to do the right thing. I basically asked her to marry me, though I fell short of using those exact words. The fact is, I loved Carolyn and I wanted to spend the rest of my life with her. I thought this would be a good place to start, and I didn't give a damn about Tyler anymore. As far as I was concerned, he didn't exist, and nothing had ever happened between him and Carolyn: it had all been a figment of my tortured imagination. All I wanted was for our relationship to go back to the way it was before Milan.

"We can make this work," I said.

"How?" she said, shaking her head from side to side, defeated. "How are we going to make this work? How are we going to survive?"

She had a point. I'd made ten thousand dollars on that Saks shoot, which was a new high for me, but I hadn't booked anything comparable since. While five thousand dollars a day sounds pretty rich, it doesn't add up to much if you're only booking two days a month.

"I love you," I said. "We'll manage."

She tried to pull herself together, and for a moment even seemed to be considering what I'd just said. She told me she didn't need much. A little house on the beach—not a mansion—with a white picket fence and maybe an old Jeep so she could feel the wind in her hair when she drove into town to run errands and get groceries. I guess the image touched her, because suddenly there were tears in her eyes.

"You don't even have medical insurance," she said. "Do you know how expensive it is to raise a child?"

"We'll be fine," I said. "The campaign's launching next month. It'll change everything." The CK underwear campaign was indeed moving forward as planned. I'd been told to brace myself for a very big and very public launch.

"Oh Michael, come on!" She was frustrated. "It's not going to happen that quickly or easily. You can't support a family. You don't know where your next job is coming from."

"Who cares?" I said. "Other people manage with less. We can do it. I know we can."

I did everything except get down on one knee.

"Stop saying that," Carolyn said. "Just stop! Please! I beg you." She stood up, moved past me, locked herself in her tiny bathroom, and began to cry in earnest. I could hear her muffled sobs through the closed door, but she wouldn't let me help her. The following Tuesday, she went to see her gynecologist. He told her that she was ten weeks pregnant. Ten weeks? I did the math and the numbers didn't add up.

"Carolyn," I said. "I was in Milan ten weeks ago." She looked up at me, and I saw a flash of concern in her eyes, but she recovered quickly.

"You're doing it again," she said, trying to keep the edge out of her voice. "There's only you. No one else. It's yours. What can I do to convince you? Maybe the doctor said eight weeks. Maybe I heard wrong. It's not like it's an exact science anyway. Want me to call him? Want it in writing?"

The heart wants what it wants. And I wanted to believe.

The next day, I tried to reach her between setups—I was doing a shoot for *Cosmopolitan*—but she wasn't at work or at home. I began to worry. On the way home, I stopped by her apartment and rang the buzzer, but there wasn't any answer. So I walked back to my place and there she was, on my red futon, under the covers, looking pale and drawn. I knew right away that she'd had the abortion.

"Jesus Christ," I said.

"I'm sorry," she said.

"Why?" I said. "I would have blown off this shitty one-day job. I would have gone with you. I didn't even know you'd made up your mind about this."

She just shook her head. She looked devastated. And I *felt* devastated. I knew it wasn't my choice, but I felt awful about the way she'd gone off and done this, without even talking to me about it. It felt dirty somehow and duplicitous. Where did I fit into the picture? What role, if any, did I still play in her life?

At the end of another week on my red futon that was strangely similar to the last postabortion week, she pulled herself together and we got on with this business of living. We'd taken a few hits—Milan, Tyler, the mistrust, this second abortion—but we were still hopeful. We kept trying. We wanted to make it.

We went up to see her mother again. She and Richard had moved to a house in New Canaan that was even more beautiful than the one in Greenwich. We went to their private club and took a long walk on the beach. She gave me a Counting Crows cassette, and told me she loved the song "Anna Begins." I racked my brain to make sense of the lyrics:

THE OTHER MAN | 157

It's chasing me away She disappears and
Oh lord, I'm not ready for this sort of thing

Nothing made sense. Even my *life* didn't make sense. I had booked the most coveted campaign in Calvin Klein's history, and I was still waiting for the launch. Meanwhile I wasn't getting any work. Zip. Zero. I was pissed at my agency. Maybe if the bookers had tried a little harder, I would've been further along. And maybe if I'd been further along, I wouldn't have been walking along the beach with my unhappy girlfriend; I would have been walking along the beach with my happy wife.

I left Click and decided to try my luck with Wilhelmina, a competing agency.

I was determined to turn my life around.

5.

Fifty Feet Tall

For a good man fame is always a problem.
—Graham Greene, *A Burnt-Out Case*

On April 28, 1994, a ninety-six-foot-tall, seventy-foot-wide bill-board went up in Times Square. I was fifty feet tall, in nothing but by my Calvin Klein briefs. People said you could see my crotch in New Jersey.

I went down to have a look and was overwhelmed. I was *huge*. I ran home and called my parents. "Mom, Dad—you've got to see this!" I blurted, barely able to contain myself. "It's unreal."

I got the same reaction as last time. "That's nice, honey."

But a week later they got a call from a friend of theirs who had been to the city. "There's a billboard of your son in Times Square," he said. "It is without a doubt the biggest billboard I've seen in my entire life."

My mother called. "Why didn't you tell us?" she asked.

"Mom," I said, laughing. "I've been telling you. You just weren't listening."

They came into the city a week later. It was a cold day, but we went down to Times Square, and they stood out in the busy street and looked up at me, towering over them. They were stunned. It really was surreal. Then I flagged a cab and we raced down to Macy's, in Herald Square, where I was making a personal appearance with Kate Moss.

The place was mobbed. Security guards had to help us through. There was a table set up at one end of the lobby, and Kate was already there. I went over, gave her a hello kiss, and sat down next to her. (I didn't have to bring an eight-by-ten this time; she remembered me.) A moment later, the guards opened the doors and the crazed fans came rushing though. Most of them were there for Kate, of course. She'd been around a lot longer than I had, and she was a known commodity. Young men arrived clutching their briefs and boxer shorts, and she autographed them with a Magic Marker. Before long, however, some of the fans began paying attention to me too. They were mostly guys, and they were all gay, but I didn't care. I signed away. For the first time in my life, I had my own fans, and I felt like a rock star. I looked toward the back of the room and saw my parents, beaming at me. They were proud. Confused, I guess, but proud. This was a long way from Naugatuck.

When it was over—when the fans and the paparazzi had all left, when the show was over, when we'd run out of eight-by-tens to sign—my mother began to cry.

"What's wrong, Ma?" I asked.

"I don't know," she said. "I'm just happy." My father shook my hand. He didn't know what to say, but it didn't matter. I could see that he was proud of me, and I felt pretty choked up.

In the days ahead I was so busy, I didn't even have time to think about Carolyn. We'd check in on the phone from time to time, but I was always rushing off. One morning I found myself back in Times Square, with a crew from *Entertainment Tonight*. The show had me stopping people on the street, within view of the billboard. I would ask them what they thought of the billboard, and if they knew who that guy was. With most people, it took a few moments.

"If that guy on the billboard was here today," I'd ask them, "standing in front of you, what would you say to him?"

"I would say . . . I would say . . ." And this was always followed by the epiphany: "It's you! *You're* the guy on the billboard! Oh my God, can I take my picture with you?" Needless to say, it was a blast. It was my first brush with celebrity, and—say what you will—I really liked it.

The whole experience was very seductive. For the first time in my life, I felt comfortable in front of a camera. This was film (or video anyway). This *moved*. It made me come alive and feel alive. In short, I wasn't just a set of abs.

Carolyn came over the following night to watch the *ET* segment on TV. I was a little nervous, understandably, but she was blown away. She was literally sitting there with her mouth hanging open. There was one sequence where I was making fun of myself and making people laugh that was full of energy, and it was easy to see that I was having the time of my life.

"I cannot believe this," she said, still in awe. "I am going to get a copy of that segment and put it on Calvin's desk."

"Why?" I said.

"Calvin needs to see this."

Unfortunately, I didn't see much of anything for a few weeks. I went up for a lot of jobs, but I didn't get them. "People are reluctant to hire someone who is so closely identified with Calvin Klein," my new booker told me. "But don't worry. Something will come along."

The whole thing was really bizarre. People saw my face and body all over the world—on billboards, on the sides of buses, in newspapers and magazines—and they assumed I was not only famous but also rich. What they didn't realize was that I'd been paid five thousand dollars for that campaign. Two days at twenty-five hundred a day, remember? And that was it. Not a penny more.

Calvin Klein spent tens of millions using me to promote its product, and all I got out of it—after agent's fees and taxes—was about two thousand bucks. Of course there were a lot of guys—including me—who would have paid just to have a shot at that campaign, but that wasn't doing me much good at the time. The company's attitude, right or wrong, was that it had made me, that any day now I'd be capitalizing on my newfound fame. But that day was a long time coming.

In the meantime, I was made painfully aware of another aspect of the modeling business. There weren't any *male* supermodels. You never heard about male models landing multimillion dollar contracts, but the females landed them every day. The fashion world, with a few exceptions, is run by men. But the female models, with *no* exceptions, were the stars. The men were a dime a dozen.

I had been in this business for a year and a half. In my first full year of modeling, I had made eighty thousand dollars. I thought that was pretty respectable, but it wasn't going to buy a house on the beach, not even a little cottage. In fact, I realized just how little it would buy when I went off to see an accountant to file my taxes. He said I owed Uncle Sam thirty-three thousand dollars. There was no way around it. I could've probably written off the occasional haircut, some of my clothes, a few beauty products, and maybe even a pair of underwear or two, but I wasn't all that good about keeping receipts, and he said it wasn't worth the risk. I paid my tax bill and was left with nothing. And I mean that literally: *nothing*.

I felt terrible and frightened. This modeling thing sucked. I thought maybe I could break into acting. Then I realized that every male model must have been entertaining that same ridiculous thought.

This was the spring of 1994, and I was seriously depressed. I was broke, I wasn't working, and I didn't even have enough money in my account to cover next month's rent. My modeling career certainly hadn't lasted very long. I saw less and less of Carolyn, and when I did, my bad moods poisoned everything. I suddenly found myself thinking about moving back home to Connecticut.

One afternoon, I was literally going through my closets, tossing stuff I didn't need, getting ready to pack my bags, when the phone rang. It was my booker. I'd just nailed a job for Coty, a perfume commercial. TV, not print. It paid $115,000.

Yes! There *is* a God!

The company flew me to White Sands, New Mexico, where I spent three days dancing on the sand with a beautiful woman. We even danced upside down one day, hanging from a crane. It was the easiest money I had ever made. The woman was nice too, though of course nothing happened. I was being faithful to Carolyn, or at least the *idea* of Carolyn—a fantasy that seemed to be on life support.

Strangely enough, she called White Sands every day. I didn't get it. When I was home, around the corner from her, she never called. But now that I was unavailable, and hanging out with a beautiful model, she needed to talk to me. "When are you coming back?" "What's going on down there?" "Why haven't you called?" "Where were you last night?"

When I returned to New York, we took up again. Sort of. I was sleeping at her place three or four nights a week, but we never went out together. I didn't even feel like showing up at any of her work-related events.

"What's wrong?" she asked.

"Nothing," I said.

But the truth was, I really didn't mind not being seen in public with her. She worked for Calvin Klein, and I didn't want people to think that she'd been instrumental in getting me the underwear gig. She'd had nothing to do with it. I knew that and she knew that, but the rest of the world might not see it the same way. Plus, I was used to being relegated to the background. It didn't faze me anymore. I'd been hidden for so long that it came naturally to me.

A few weeks later, ironically enough, her efforts on my behalf paid off: Calvin had finally taken a look at the *ET* tape, and he had reacted just as she had expected he would. He loved it; he loved *me*. Suddenly he was thinking of me for everything: underwear, jeans, suits, even the Escape fragrance campaign.

In June, I did another CK shoot with Kate Moss. She was dating Johnny Depp at the time, and, once again, she didn't want to make her boyfriend jealous. But the photographer, Tiziano Magni, had his own agenda.

"I want you to get on top of Kate and pretend you're fucking the shit out of her," he told me. "I mean really grind the shit out of her." It was pretty crude. I didn't feel like grinding, and Kate didn't feel like being ground, so we tried to compromise.

The entire thing was insane. I remember standing around in my underwear while they were setting up the lights when this gay guy came over, reached inside my crotch, and grabbed my penis like it was a piece of meat.

"Hey!" I screamed at him. "What the fuck are you doing?"

"Hey yourself!" he shouted back. "That's my job. I'm the stylist. I have to style your penis too."

"I can style my own penis, thank you very much."

"You're not being very professional, Michael."

"Just tell me where you want my penis, and how you want it to look. I can take care of it myself. My penis and I understand each other."

We got through the shoot, and it looked great. Calvin liked it so much that he decided to let me do the suit campaign. Oddly enough, Tyler had done the most recent suit campaign, but now he was gone: my nemesis was history. I was the new CK suit guy. It felt great. Carolyn was really coming through for me. I didn't think there was anything wrong with that. I actually thought she was working for us both, that maybe we could still get back on track, that we had a future. I began to think about that house on the beach with the white picket fence. I could smell the salt in the air.

My career really began to take off. I did commercials and print ads for Bacardi rum, L'Oréal, Kellogg's, Maybelline, Perry Ellis, Claiborne, and a host of overseas designers I had never even heard of. I found myself shooting with some amazing photographers: Herb Ritts. Arthur Elgort. Greg Gorman. John Falocco. I was making real money—not supermodel money, but enough to pay the bills and even save a little.

I didn't have a Porsche, and there still weren't any limos, but I was doing well and feeling good. Not that I got any respect, mind you. As a male model, I was defined by my looks. People assumed I didn't have a brain. And even when they realized that I did, they weren't interested in what I thought. I was product, a set of abs, a human coat hanger, a crotch, an ass in a pair of tight jeans. Okay. Fine. I'd signed up for this, I could take it. But I still resented it a little. I had met a lot of models who weren't the brightest bulbs in town, but most of them were just regular, college-educated guys who were better looking than the average citizen and had decided to capitalize on their God-given gifts.

Yet when someone finally did get around to seeing me as a human being, it was usually a member of the press, and that never worked out the way I expected. It took me a while to figure out that most reporters only heard what they wanted to hear, and *how* they wanted to hear it. I remember one interviewer asking me if I was good in bed, and I laughed and joked, "Oh sure, I'm *great* in bed. I'm as good as it gets." And the son of a bitch wrote it as if I meant it. Ask me how I felt when I read that. Ask me how my mother felt. I wish I had learned something from those experiences, but I kept hoping that the next reporter would actually tell the truth. I was almost always disappointed.

As for Carolyn, it was hard to figure out what was going on. Once again, the relationship felt like it was winding down, though neither of us would acknowledge it. Of course Carolyn had never been eager to define it as a relationship. It had always been this *thing.* I'd never known exactly what, and I knew even less now. [It's like the old saying about the tree in the woods: if no one is there to hear it fall, has it made a sound? Did the tree (or the relationship) even exist?]

It struck me that it's true what they say: in work there is escape. I worked and she worked, and we seemed to be escaping each other. We were still seeing each other, yes, but only in bed, in private, and with much less frequency. There was still plenty of passion there of course, and mutual hunger, but everything felt somehow diminished, as if it were winding down. I didn't like the feeling.

One night, missing her, I reached her in the office to see about hooking up. But she was busy. She had a party to go to at Nell's, and Kate Moss was supposed to make an appearance on behalf of Calvin Klein. I wondered why she didn't invite me. It pissed me off.

I called up Nicole. You remember Nicole, right? The exotic dancer. She was dating Gabriel, a male model, and we had remained friends. On the phone anyway. So I called her and discovered that she knew all about the party. Gabriel had been invited, and he was going, but he hadn't asked Nicole to go along.

"Why don't we go?" she said.

And I said, "Why not?"

When we arrived, Gabriel was nowhere in sight, but Carolyn was standing around, talking to a model I knew only fleetingly. Nicole and I brushed right past them, I smiled my friendliest smile, said hello to both Carolyn and her friend, and kept walking.

Nicole and I stood at the bar, and I ordered two shots of tequila. I fought the urge to turn around and look at Carolyn. I knew she was watching us, and I was curious about the way our entrance had affected her.

Nicole reached for a cigarette. There were dozens of small candles lined up and down the bar, in tiny glass dishes, and I reached for one to light Nicole's cigarette. Before I had even set the candle down, Carolyn was at my side, literally shoving Nicole out of the way.

"Can I talk to you?" she said through clenched teeth. But she didn't even wait for an answer. She dragged me to the nearest corner, pinned me to the wall, and took my face in her hands, literally burying her fingernails into my skin. "What the fuck do you think you're doing?" she hissed. "And what the hell is *she* doing here?"

I was mortified. People were staring. Nicole was looking over at us in stunned disbelief. "Carolyn," I said, getting pretty steamed myself, "this isn't cool." I pulled away and crossed back to the bar, and Nicole decided it was *her* turn to rip me a new asshole.

"You'd better get your bitch girlfriend under control!" she said, then reached for one of the candles and threw it on the ground, shattering the dish. She did this a second time and then a third, and suddenly Gordon showed up and intervened before she could shatter a fourth.

"What the hell is going on?" Gordon said.

By this time we were getting a lot of attention. We were a regular floor show.

I turned and caught a glimpse of my face in a mirror. I had two bloody slits on each cheek from where Carolyn's nails had burst through the skin. Behind me, also reflected in the mirror, I saw a pair of security guards hurrying toward us. I turned as they reached our side, and wanted to explain, but they weren't in a talkative mood. One of them pinned my arm behind my back and escorted me to the door, and guess what? I didn't resist. I was relieved—glad to get the hell out of there. I flagged a passing cab, jumped in, and went home, but I'd barely made it through the door when the buzzer sounded.

"Who is it?" I said.

"It's me," Carolyn said. I didn't want to let her up, but she buzzed again and again and wouldn't stop until I let her through. She walked in, fuming. I had never seen such rage in her eyes.

"What is wrong with you?!" she screamed, and she punched me in the chest with her small fists. *Boom, boom, boom*—three times in quick succession.

"Carolyn—"

"How dare you parade that girl around in front of me?!"

She turned, saw one of my white candles—a *huge* candle, nothing like the little ones back at the bar, candles I'd purchased to protect myself from evil spirits—picked it up, and flung it across the room. She threw it so hard that she chipped the plaster on the wall.

"Carolyn!"

I began to move toward her, but she was already reaching for candle number two, and I ducked as it flew past and shattered the window that looked out onto the courtyard. Then she threw a third, striking the mirror over the mantel—the mirror we'd bought together at the flea market—and smashed it to bits. The shards rained down on the floor. There was one candle left. She threw it at my feet, and it gouged a two-inch hunk out of the polished wood floor.

"What is wrong with you?!" she screamed, completely losing control. "You like trashy girls?! Is that it? You like them dirty?"

She turned and kicked my TV set, knocking the VCR to the ground, then she literally leapt into the air and came crashing down on the VCR, smashing it. I didn't want to be there, and I didn't know how to stop her without manhandling her, so I did what any sane man would have done in a similar situation: I ran. I tore through the door, down two flights of stairs, and out into the street. I was running like a marathoner, really goddamn moving, but the next thing I knew Carolyn was on my ass, and she was *gaining* on me. She was moving like lightning. This was nuts!

"You little baby!" she was screaming. "What's the matter? Can't you take it? Are you running away from me, wimp? Run, little baby, run!"

I don't know what came over me—the rage, the adrenaline, her craziness—but I stopped on a dime, turned, and pushed her with all my might. And Christ if her body didn't go flying. Carolyn was not a small girl, but she literally left the ground, sailed through the air, and landed on a nearby stoop. I couldn't believe what I'd done. I hurried over.

"Carolyn?" I said.

She didn't say anything. She looked stunned and seemed to be trying to get her bearings. I sat down next to her. "You okay?" She still looked numb and lost, but she nodded. I put my arm around her shoulders and said I was sorry, and she rested her head against my chest. We sat there for a while, the two of us, confused and emptied out, and after a few minutes I stood and walked her back to my apartment. We went upstairs, dropped onto the red futon, and made perhaps the most passionate love of our lives. We were burning up for each other. We didn't talk. What was there to say? Both of us were crazy. We were making each other crazy.

She left early the next morning, before I was up. We drifted apart again, and I lost myself in my work. We'd call each other from time to time, but even during those calls we felt as if we were talking to each other from a great distance, as if it was already over and we both knew it but remained unwilling to let go.

At the end of July, I was preparing to leave for Europe again.

This time she wasn't there to help me shop or tell me what I needed, but it didn't matter. I already knew what I needed: she had taught me well. I went to Milan again. To Paris. I was a known entity now—the underwear guy—and I stayed in better hotels, closer to the action. But I was still one of the male models. No limos for me, no little gifts waiting for me on the pillow. I was on billboards and buses and in subway stations—but I was still just one of the guys.

When I returned from Europe, I called Carolyn again. She was busy. She had to go to the Hamptons that weekend and again the following weekend and again the weekend after that. She was hanging out with Calvin and Kelly. "They need me," she said. "They're having problems."

In an odd way, I think my success had begun to frighten her a little. Up until very recently, I had always been there for her, and I would come running at a moment's notice. And I think Carolyn needed that, needed to know that I was there and always would be. I don't think there was anything calculating or malicious about it; I simply think it's who she was. Now that I was harder to reach, now that I was less available, she was going to make a concerted effort to want me less. Consciously or not, she was distancing herself from me.

"I need you too," I said. I asked her to please take one weekend and come to Naugatuck, to visit my family with me, but she said she couldn't—not now. I didn't know what was going on with the Calvin and Kelly, and I didn't ask. And I certainly wasn't thinking that anything else might be going on: with JFK Jr., for example. Months ago, I'd read in the *Post* that he was dating Daryl Hannah and that they were very happy.

But this was the summer of 1994, and Jacqueline Kennedy had passed away the previous May. Now I was reading that John Jr. and Daryl Hannah were finished, that Jackie had never approved of

Daryl, and that John had dumped her as way of showing respect for his late mother.

At the same time, I heard that John was hanging out in the Hamptons, as a guest of Calvin and Kelly. Coincidence? I didn't think so. I called Carolyn and asked her about it, though I'm not sure I had the right to ask. "He's just a friend," she said. "And he's going through a lot."

"I'm going through a lot too," I said. "I miss you."

I went up to Naugatuck the following weekend to see my parents. They were leaving to vacation in Ireland, and I wanted to wish them well. After they left, I hung out visiting with Tommy and the gang, and stayed at the house Sunday night.

I slept well past noon on Monday, and when I woke up, I made myself a cup of coffee, dropped onto the living room couch, and turned on the TV. *A Current Affair* was on. The first thing I heard was a teaser—something about JFK Jr.'s new love—then it cut to a commercial.

I thought this was pretty funny. "Hey, Tina," I hollered to my sister. "Get this! They're doing a segment on JFK's new girlfriend." She came out to the living room and joined me. I was grinning. "Watch. It'll turn out to be Carolyn."

I was kidding of course. Despite all evidence to the contrary, I believed Carolyn. *Nothing is going on with John Jr. He's a friend. You have nothing to worry about.* But suddenly, *A Current Affair* was back on, and it was flashing a picture of John Jr. on a boat at Martha's Vineyard. With Carolyn. *My* Carolyn. I was in total shock. Carolyn was wearing a T-shirt and something that looked suspiciously like underwear, and John Jr. seemed to be helping her into her pants.

"Jesus," I said. I felt physically ill.

Tina looked over at me. "Oh, Michael," she said, covering her face with her hands.

I watched the rest of the segment. It gave a quick bio on Carolyn—publicist at Calvin Klein, Connecticut born and bred, blond hair, blue eyes, and supremely elegant—then it mentioned Daryl Hannah and the recent death of John's mother. I left the room, grabbed the phone, and called Carolyn at work. She wasn't there, but I kept trying until I reached her. I was beside myself.

"Did you see what I just saw on *A Current Affair*?"

"No," she said.

"It's fascinating," I said. "You're the new woman in JFK Jr.'s life. You're out on a boat with him at Martha's Vineyard, but you tell me you're with Calvin and Kelly in the Hamptons."

"That's such bullshit, Michael," she said. But she said it without much conviction. I was suddenly furious. I realized how naive I'd been, and why I'd allowed myself to be so naive. Love really does make you blind.

"You look very happy together," I said.

"How many times do I have to tell you, Michael?" she said. "He's a friend, and he's going through a difficult time."

"Really? He didn't look like he was suffering too much. And neither did you."

I hung up, got a beer out of the fridge, called my friend Tommy, and went out and got drunk in earnest. On Tuesday morning, still at my parents', I woke up with a pounding hangover. Tommy had passed out on the couch and looked equally hungover.

"Let's get the hell out of here," I said. "Let's go on a trip."

I dug up some aspirin and a newspaper and found a great deal to Cancún. Airfare, transportation, and hotel—an entire week for $299. I didn't realize it was hurricane season, but even if I had, I wouldn't have cared. Let a goddamn hurricane blow me out to sea!

I called my booker and told her not to schedule anything for the week. I was going out of town.

"Where are you going?" she said.

"Cancún," I said. "Why don't you come with us? It's just me and my buddy Tommy."

She was actually taking the rest of the week off to see some relatives, but this sounded better. So she switched her plans around, and we booked her on our flight.

Tommy and I met her at the airport. He had a nice buzz going, and I was already smashed. I pounded drinks all the way to Cancún and drank myself into a stupor for the next six nights. I had tequila oozing out of my eyeballs. I never looked so bad in my life. One drunken night I slept with my booker, and the next night I slept with a girl I picked up on the beach. Oh, yeah—I was in fine shape! I didn't miss Carolyn at all! I wasn't even thinking about her.

That's what I told myself, but I couldn't get that one picture of her out of my head: Carolyn, on the boat, in her underwear, with John helping her into her pants. It was seared into my brain. I tried to drink it away, but it never left. I must have listened to that Counting Crows tape about four hundred times that week.

I got off the plane in New York, still drunk, and there were more pictures of them at the airport newsstands. Carolyn and John; John and Carolyn. Prince Charming and his Beautiful Blond Princess.

What an idiot I'd been! Carolyn had never acknowledged that she'd ever had sex with *anyone*. She could never say, "I slept with him" or "We had a little fling." She could have made it sound classy if she wanted to; she could have referred to a *brief liaison* if that made her feel better. But no. Not Carolyn. To Carolyn, every man was a friend.

Pictures of Carolyn and JFK Jr. started appearing in both the tabloid press and the more legitimate newspapers. Here they were leaving a movie theater. Here they were having lunch at a sidewalk café. And here they were kissing in Central Park. That one in Central Park really got to me. Not only were they kissing in public, but she was holding on to him like she really meant it. I hooked up with Gordon the following week.

"How do I compete with that?" I asked him. "I'm a fucking underwear model. He's American Royalty."

"I hear he can't get it up," Gordon said.

"You're sick," I said.

"That's what I hear," he said, but he was smiling, and I think he was just messing with my head. "I hear they had a big argument on Fifth Avenue, and she left him crying on the curb."

I gave it a week, then finally broke down and called. "So what's going on?" I asked. I didn't ask her whether we were finished, because the answer seemed obvious, and I didn't want her to confirm it. I still, foolishly, had hope.

"Nothing," she said. "We're just friends."

I was glad we were on the phone. If she'd been there in person, I don't know what I would have done. *Friends who just happen to kiss each other in public. Friends who spend weekends together in Martha's Vineyard and the Hamptons.*

"What are you doing this weekend?" I asked. What can I say? I was weak and needy.

"I'm going to the Hamptons again," she said.

"Is he going to be there?"

"I don't know."

"How did this happen?" I said. "I turn around for a minute and suddenly JFK Jr. is your best friend."

"It isn't what you think," she said. But she didn't know what I thought. And she never told me what "it" was. And then she had to get off the phone; she was swamped with work. "Don't believe everything you read in the papers," she said, and she hung up.

I kept drinking. I picked up two different women and brought them home to Mom on two consecutive weekends. I don't know what I was trying to prove. That I didn't care? That I wasn't hurt?

Mom was not amused. We were relegated to the L-shaped couch in the living room.

Then summer came and it was showtime again. My phone rang. It was Carolyn, calling me out of the blue.

"Hey," she said.

"Hey," I said.

"Want to come over?"

Of course I didn't want to come over. She'd lied to me. She'd broken my heart.

I went over. She opened the door and half hugged me and smiled self-consciously. "You look great," she said. She was lying again. I looked like shit. I'd barely survived that drinking binge. "How's it going?"

"Okay," I said.

"I hear everything's really going well for you."

"Yeah," I said.

"That's great," she said.

Suddenly the buzzer sounded. Carolyn crossed to the wall. "Hello," she said.

"It's me," a man said. It was John Jr. His voice was clear and unmistakable. Carolyn turned to look at me, calm and unruffled. "Would you do me a favor?" she asked. "Would you go down and wait for me at our bagel place?" Nice touch, that *our* bagel place.

"Sure," I said.

"Would you mind taking the stairs, sweetie?"

I felt sick to my stomach. John Jr. was on his way up in the elevator, and I was sneaking down the back stairs like a goddamn criminal.

I waited at the bagel place. After twenty minutes, she walked in, and I was steamed.

"Don't look at me like that," she said.

"How am I supposed to look at you?"

"I just didn't want him to get the wrong idea," she said.

"But it's okay for me to get the wrong idea?" I asked. "Or no idea at all?"

She looked so deeply hurt that I felt bad. I felt manipulated, yes, and I felt like a fool; but I still felt bad. It occurred to me that Carolyn and I hadn't been together for almost two months now, and that I really had no right to question her like this. Ironic, isn't it? If she wasn't going to make excuses for herself, I was only too happy to make them for her. So, okay. He was her guy now, and I was the other man.

"Please don't hate me," she said.

"I don't hate you," I said. And I didn't. I really didn't. Carolyn had been more than a lover. She'd been a best friend, an adviser, a guide, an angel. How could I possibly hate her?

6.

Life Without Carolyn

With love one can live even without happiness.
—Dostoyevsky, "Bookishness and Literacy"

In November of 1994, I went back to Europe for another tour of the fashion capitals. I didn't find it particularly exciting, even now, with my modicum of celebrity, but it kept my mind off Carolyn.

When I was in Paris, I saw Valentino again. I went over to his suite at the Ritz for drinks, and I told him all about Carolyn. He was like a second father to me. He could see that I was badly hurt, and he went out of his way to keep me occupied. He dragged me to various events and a number of fancy dinners. I drank too much and worked too hard at forgetting Carolyn by having sex with women I didn't know and didn't want.

I stayed in Paris for several weeks, hoping to crack that market and trying to mend my broken heart, but finally it was time to get on a plane and fly back to New York. Before I knew it, Christmas had come, and I went home to my family. The day after I arrived I got a call from Carolyn, right there at my parents' place. She told me she was in Woodbury, for a party at her uncle's house, and asked if I would come. The words just sort of spilled out of her.

"I don't know," I said. "Do you want me to?"

"I wouldn't be asking if I didn't want you to," she said, using my own words from long ago, from when I'd first invited her to Naugatuck.

Her uncle was a dentist in Woodbury, which was only twenty minutes away, so I went. There was good wine and plenty to eat, and everyone was very nice, but before long Carolyn and I drifted off and found ourselves alone at the far end of the house. This wing contained the dental office, with that big leather chair and all the shiny equipment. I sat in the chair and Carolyn looked at me like she wanted to kiss me. It made me think of the movie *Marathon Man*: the scene where Laurence Olivier uses his ominous-looking dental tools to torture Dustin Hoffman, and I was Hoffman. I was there as Carolyn's friend, not her lover, and it hurt. But it was better than no Carolyn at all.

"How are you?" she asked.

"Okay," I said. "How come you called?"

"Can't I call?" she said. "I missed you."

"What will these people think?" I said.

"I don't care what they think," she said.

I wanted to ask her about John, but I didn't. We went back out, and mingled and ate until it was time for me to go home. Carolyn walked me out to my blue Honda and was pinching my forearm in that fidgety way of hers. As I unlocked the car, she got a look of panic in her eyes.

"Why do you have to go?" she said.

"What would you like me to do?" I said. She just looked at me. There are women who don't like to ask for things, who like their men to figure them out on their own, and Carolyn was one of those women. "You want me to stay a little longer?"

"Would you?" she said, but her heart wasn't in it.

"You want to come back to Naugatuck with me?"

Her eyes sparkled. "Could I?"

"Sure," I said.

"I have to be at my parents' house in the morning."

"I can take you," I said.

"I'll be right back," she said and she went to the house to get her things and say good-bye to her family. I again wondered what they must be thinking, but it wasn't my business, and I decided not to worry about it. In any event, they were Carolyn's family, not mine.

We drove to Naugatuck and got there just as my parents were getting ready for bed. They were surprised to see Carolyn, but they hid it well. Here she was—John Jr.'s Blond Princess—and it was confusing for all concerned. But my family adored Carolyn; I think they were still upset that it hadn't worked out for us.

We stayed on the L-shaped couch. I killed the lights and kissed her good night—a short, chaste kiss. I don't know what she was thinking as she drifted off, but I was thinking about how much I wanted her. She reached for me. We ended up on the floor, under the Christmas tree, but nothing happened.

In the morning, after breakfast, I drove her back to Greenwich. I didn't even go inside. I said good-bye to her at the front door, turned around, got back into my Honda, and headed home.

I didn't hear from her over the next few days, and I didn't think it was my place to call. Suddenly it was a new year, 1995, and I was back working in Manhattan. I was determined to get on with my life, without Carolyn. Then one day, shortly before my birthday, I found a package waiting for me outside my apartment. It was a beautiful antique birdcage from Carolyn. She had left a note, wishing me the very best. I called to thank her, but I never heard back. I felt bereft all over again. Part of me wished she'd just leave me alone.

In March, I got invited to the Academy Awards, but not as a guest. Mel Gibson's *Braveheart* had received several nominations, including one for costume design. I was one of the models that pranced around onstage in a *Braveheart* costume. It wasn't as pathetic as it sounds. This was the Academy Awards, after all. You couldn't turn around without bumping into a star. I shook Mel Gibson's hand, said hi to Sharon Stone, met John Travolta—one of my heroes. I was walking on air. *This is where I belong,* I thought. *This is where I want to be.*

Before the night was over, however, I came down from the clouds, and I came down *hard*. I'd been struggling from acute stomach pain for the better part of two weeks, but I'd been so busy that I chose to ignore it. By the time I left the Shrine Auditorium, however, I couldn't ignore it anymore. I was literally doubled over in pain. By morning, I was in pure agony. Somehow I found the strength to get to the airport and crawl on to my New York flight. I suffered through five excruciating hours, landed, took a cab into Manhattan, dumped my bags at my apartment, and immediately took a second cab to Lenox Hill Hospital.

The news was not good. My small intestine was dangerously inflamed, and the doctors were forced to operate right away. They removed part of the intestine, which was already seriously infected, along with my appendix, which was also infected. When I woke up in the recovery room, I was told I probably had Crohn's disease, a chronic condition marked by inflammation of the bowels. There was no known cure, the doctor said, but many people had long periods of remission, sometimes for years on end. If I was lucky, I would be one of those people.

I went to Naugatuck to recuperate, but the pain was so intense that my mother had to drive me to the local hospital for morphine. I have never felt such pain in my life, and I wouldn't wish it on my worst enemy.

A few weeks later, fully recovered, I got a call from Candace Bushnell. She had a column in the newspaper called "Sex and the City," which later inspired the huge hit for HBO. She was a friend of Tad

Small, my manager, and she wanted to interview me for the column. She thought it would make a fun story: "A Day in Manhattan with the Calvin Klein Underwear Guy."

She was on her way over on the appointed day when it began to pour. She was drenched when she got to my apartment, so I lent her a towel, and she managed to dry off a little. I was a little embarrassed to have her there. I was supposed to be this famous model, and I lived in a tiny one-room studio. She didn't seem to mind. She sat on the edge of the bed and said we could talk right there. She started asking me questions about my life—where I was born, how I got into modeling, how I liked it—but then she noticed a little wooden box on the mantel.

"What's that?" she asked.

I showed her. It had been a gift from a friend. There was a little pipe inside with a cleverly designed area in which to store pot. The pot still was still there, untouched. I wasn't a big drug user.

"Let's smoke it," she said.

We got pretty high, and I found myself telling her more than I wanted to. I told her that Tad called me the Bone. "He thinks I'm a walking penis," I explained, "but he's wrong. I'm actually kind of shy around women. And I prefer sex that's about more than sex." It was true. I had made my share of mistakes—I had slept with women I hadn't really cared about, especially recently—but that wasn't the real me. The real me preferred an emotional connection.

"Well, I like you," she said. "I think we have an emotional connection."

The next thing you know, we were tearing off each other's clothes and going at it. She spent the night, and we went at it again in the morning, and then we went our separate ways.

Tad called me later in the day and asked me how the interview had gone. "Fine," I said. And he asked, "You didn't sleep with her, did you?" And I told him no, of course not, what did he think I was?

A few days later, Valentino was in town. He called me and I went over for dinner. We were good friends, but I never knew what to expect at his house. For example, on a subsequent visit to his home, I had drinks with Hugh Grant and Elizabeth Hurley. After everyone had been served, Valentino took us into the den and put a cassette into his VCR. It was a tape of Pamela Anderson and Tommy Lee screwing on a yacht. It was pretty raunchy. We were all snickering nervously.

I liked Valentino. I told him after dinner that night that I was going up to Naugatuck for the weekend and invited him along. I said I wanted him to meet my family. I thought he'd get a kick out of seeing where I was from. Amazingly enough, he agreed to come. A few Sundays later, he came up in a limo. My mother was a nervous wreck. She had decided to make lasagna, because he was Italian, and then it occurred to her that he ate Italian food all the time, and that she probably should have made something more American. But it was too late. There he was now, at our front door. He brought my mother a beautiful cashmere scarf and we sat in the living room and chatted, then we "repaired" to the dining room for dinner. Valentino passed on the lasagna; I think he wasn't big on meat or cheese. My mother was crushed, but he joked with her and picked at the rest of the food, and before long she was back in fine spirits.

"I can't believe it," my mother whispered to me as the evening was winding down. "*Valentino.* In *my* house. It's amazing."

I walked Valentino to his limo. "Michael," he said. "You have a wonderful family. You are a very lucky man. I hope you know that."

Tad heard about Valentino's visit and went a little berserk. What was a world-famous designer doing driving out to Naugatuck to meet the parents of a model? He came over to my apartment and interrogated me, and I explained that Valentino was like a second father to me, but he couldn't get his mind around the idea. "Are you sure?" he said.

"Tad," I said. "Are you insinuating that I've got something going with Valentino?"

"Of course not," he protested, but it was clear that the thought had crossed his mind.

"I thought you knew me," I said.

He fluttered around like a big, nervous bird. "You're not going to leave me, are you?" he asked me worriedly.

"No," I said. "You're still my manager."

The fact is, I was Tad's only client, and I liked him. He was doing a good job for me—he'd arranged two film auditions that week alone—but he was getting a little obsessed with me. He was worried that I'd dump him for a real manager, and he kept begging me not to leave. It was pretty tiresome. He began to suspect that I was plotting behind his back, and he somehow managed to get ahold of the PIN code I used to check the messages on my service. Before long I realized that he knew a little too much about my life, and that of late he had been referring to things I knew I had never shared. When I confronted him, he denied it, but I didn't believe him.

"You are not only violating my trust," I said, "but the trust of everyone who calls and leaves messages for me."

I went back to my apartment, angry, and Tad showed up later, pounding on the door, begging to be let in. I didn't want to let him in, but he was making a scene, and I was worried about the neighbors. So I opened the door. He looked like he was about to cry.

"What do you want?" I demanded.

"Nothing," he said. "I just need you to know you're wrong. I would never listen to your messages. I would never violate you like that."

"You're a fucking liar!" I shouted.

Amazingly enough, he caved almost immediately. He admitted it. He said he was sorry and promised that it would never happen again. I was so pissed I literally grabbed him and pushed him back out into the hallway. He began pounding on the door again and screaming at the top of his voice, and Tad can be *loud*. Now I was at a total loss. I had a complete madman on my hands. This felt like a *Twilight Zone* replay of the incident with Carolyn.

I grabbed my running shoes, put them on, and stepped out into the corridor. Tad thought I was going to let him in, but I pushed him aside, locked the door, and took off down the stairs. Tad came after me, but he wasn't in great shape, and I knew he wouldn't be able to keep up.

"Where are you going?" he screamed, tackling the steps.

"It's over, Tad. We're finished. You're not my manager anymore."

"After everything I've done for you!" he wailed. He was practically crying. "All the wonderful people I've introduced you to?!"

"Thanks for everything," I said over my shoulder. "Really."

When I hit the street, I began to jog. I was going at a good clip, and I turned around and saw Tad behind me, struggling to keep up. He was a good twenty pounds overweight at the time, and he had his chin thrust way out, determined, grim, and his curly mop of hair was bouncing wildly as he ran. We were almost at the corner when he spotted two uniformed cops, and he shouted at the top of his voice: "Stop that man! Officer! That man assaulted me!"

Just as I was turning the corner, the two cops started running after me. I couldn't believe it. The whole thing was ridiculous. Both of them were overweight, and everything on their leather belts was bouncing crazily: flashlights, cuffs, guns, keys. It was surreal. Three large out-of-shape men were chasing me down the street. Was I dreaming, or was this really happening?

So I stopped running; time for a reality check. The two cops caught up to me, wheezing, and literally pinned me to the wall.

"Wait a minute!" I said. "This guy is full of shit! He's my manager."

When Tad finally reached us, struggling to catch his breath, he somehow managed to get the words out. "It's all right, officers," he said, pausing for huge gulps of air. "I'm not going to press charges." The two cops were pretty pissed, and they gave Tad a hard time about enlisting their help on a personal matter. After they left, Tad came closer and looked at me with his big eyes. He looked like a tired old woman.

"Am I still your manager?" he asked.

"Are you nuts?" I said. "I never want to see you again." And I took off running.

The next thing I knew there was an item in the local gossip column about my "very close" relationship with Valentino. I suspected Tad had something to do with it, but I didn't let it bother me. If people wanted to think I was gay, let them think it. I was in a world full of gay men, I had a lot of gay friends, and gay men had always treated me with respect.

Over the next several months, I may have inadvertently fueled some of these rumors when I began getting involved in fund-raisers. I did a benefit with Christy Turlington called Seventh on Sale to raise money to fight AIDS. It was a four-day shopping extravaganza at the Twenty-sixth Street Armory in Manhattan. Then I did a poster for the DISHES Project, which raised money for pediatric AIDS. This led to more work with children, and eventually I became a national spokesman for DARE (Drug Abuse Resistance Education), the antidrug program aimed at kids. Since my father was a cop, he was very pleased.

The year was flying by. At the end of August, after yet another out-of-town fund-raiser, I got back to New York and hooked up with Gordon.

"She's living with him," he said. "She moved into his loft in Tribeca."

"I don't want to hear it," I said. I didn't want to think about Carolyn. I was trying to move on.

Two days later, on September 1, I was walking down the street, minding my own business, when I passed the newsstand near my house. And there it was on the cover of the *New York Post*: JFK JR. POPS THE QUESTION. Under that, in smaller letters, I read: GIRL-FRIEND HASN'T SAID YES . . . YET!

Part of me didn't want to believe it. I figured it was the usual tabloid bullshit. The other part of me remained oddly hopeful. She hadn't accepted. Maybe I still had a chance. There wasn't much more to the article than what they were trumpeting on the cover. It hurt. Shit like that can make a guy want to reach for a drink, but by this time I knew better. I wasn't going to fall into that trap. I was going to focus on the work.

I did some guest hosting for *ET,* VH-1, and E! Television. Then I got an actual acting job, my first real one since *Whispers in the Dark* (not that that had much to do with acting). It was on a show called *Central Park West,* created by Darren Star, who'd had so much success with *Melrose Place.* I auditioned for the part of Brad, the bartender, and I got it. That first day before the cameras, I was a nervous wreck, and I think it showed. I had a scene at the bar, where I was answering the phone and trying to look like a busy bartender. It sounded easy enough, but I was green and nervous—a deadly combination—and I didn't exactly pull it off with great flair. Unfortunately, I failed very publicly. Darren had invited the press to watch my debut, and they were trampling on each other to get a look at me on screen. I thought my acting days were over.

In December, I went out to Los Angeles for a week of catalogue work, which I was going to cap by doing another benefit, this one with Giorgio Armani. The night before the benefit, one of the bookers at Wilhelmina invited me to Brad Pitt's birthday party.

I walked in and was immediately starstruck. Brad was there with Gwyneth Paltrow, whom he was seeing at the time. Jennifer Aniston was also there, ironically, since she and Brad would eventually end up together, and so was David Schwimmer. Melissa Etheridge, who lived next door, came by to sing her own special version of "Happy Birthday."

I wanted to tell someone that I was in Brad Pitt's house, with all his famous friends, so I found my way into the kitchen and picked up the phone to call my little sister.

"Hey, Jessica," I whispered. "Guess where I am?"

"Where?" she said, annoyed; it was pretty late on the East Coast.

"I'm in Brad Pitt's kitchen," I said.

"Shut up!" she said. "I don't believe you."

"No," I said. "I really am."

At that moment, Brad himself walked into the kitchen. "Hey dude," he said and gave me a big smile. "How's it going?"

I was mortified. Here I was on Brad's phone, making a long-distance call and talking about him, and wondering what he'd heard.

"G-g-great," I stammered as my little sister screamed into my ear: "Oh my God! It *is* Brad Pitt. I heard Brad Pitt's voice. You really weren't lying! Shut up!"

When I left, Jennifer Aniston gave me a little kiss good-bye. "I'll never wash this cheek again," I told her.

That weekend, at the AIDS benefit with Armani, I took a turn on the runway and was overwhelmed by the faces in the crowd: Harrison Ford. Michelle Pfeiffer. Laura Dern. Jeff Goldblum. Steve Baldwin.

At the party afterward, I found myself putting away shots of Jack Daniel's with Stevie Baldwin, and I must have put away quite a few. When it was time to leave, I didn't actually feel drunk, so I got into my rental car and began negotiating my way back to the home of a friend, where I was staying. I was fiddling with the unfamiliar radio when a red traffic light snuck up on me, and I found myself going through it. A moment later, I saw the flashing lights behind me and pulled over. The officer put me through a sobriety test. The straight line. The finger to the nose. And, finally, the Breathalyzer. I guess I was off the charts.

"You're in trouble, pal," he said.

"Would it help if I told you my father was a cop?" I asked.

"No," he said.

He cuffed me, put me into the back of the squad car, and took me down to the station, where I waited in this little room, with my hands cuffed to a bar. There was another guy there, and he kept looking at me.

"Don't I know you?" he said.

"No," I said. "You don't."

"No," he insisted. "I'm sure I know you. You're that guy on TV." It was like a Woody Allen routine, only it wasn't funny.

The cop came to get me for my one phone call, and I called my father, half expecting him to rip me a new asshole. But he didn't. He was concerned and disappointed, but he was there for me, solid as a rock. He said that I had messed up, sure, that I'd be spending the night in jail, and that we would deal with this in the morning. I felt better just hearing his voice.

The officer finished filling out the paperwork, told me where to sign, and escorted me to the cell. It was small but clean and I dropped onto the bare mattress and passed out. Someone woke me early the next morning and sent me on my way. The rental had been towed, so I dealt with that and then went back to my friend's house to shower and call my father.

"I'm sorry," I said.

"Don't apologize to me," he said. "You did this to yourself."

My father is a wise man.

★ ★ ★

In February 1996, some paparazzi got a shot of Carolyn and JFK Jr. arguing in Washington Square Park. The picture was everywhere. The accompanying blurb claimed that Carolyn had pulled a ring off her finger and tossed it to the ground. I didn't believe it. What ring? I didn't even know she was engaged. Last I'd heard, from the usual reliable sources (the *Post* et cetera), she was still considering his marriage proposal.

I heard nothing else until the following month, when Carolyn called me unexpectedly. She seemed to have reached a breaking point: she could only go a few months without seeing me. She needed her fix.

"How are you?" she said.

"I can't complain," I said. I was working, making money, raising money for worthy causes, and taking acting classes.

"I have something for you," she said.

She came over to the apartment with a bird, a sun conure not unlike my mother's, except that it was mostly pea green. It was strange seeing her. I found it hard to look into her blue eyes. She didn't even come inside.

"Happy birthday," she said from the stoop. "It'll go nice with the antique cage I gave you last year."

"Thanks," I said, "but I can't take it. I travel all the time."

"I put a lot of thought into this," she said.

"Carolyn," I said, "I'm sure you did. And it's a beautiful bird. But who's going to take care of it?"

"I don't know," she said. "If you don't want it, take it back." She gave me the name of the pet shop and took off, fuming. I was never going to figure her out.

It was too late in the day to take the bird back, so I carried it upstairs, put it in the antique cage, and sat down to work on my taxes. I had piles of receipts to sift through, having learned my lesson about write-offs. But it was late already, so I showered, dressed, and went off to celebrate my birthday with Gordon and a group of friends, including a few buddies from Naugatuck. We met at a place called the Tunnel, on the West Side Highway, and one of my friends offered me a hit of ecstasy. It had the desired effect. When the drug kicked in, I felt the love in the room. I loved everyone. I loved all my friends. I loved all the strangers at the bar. I loved the entire god-damn world. I thought life was a truly beautiful thing.

The next morning, the bird woke me up. He was out of the cage and rummaging through my taxes like a damn auditor. Half the papers were on the floor, the other half were chewed into drooly balls.

I took him back to the pet shop. It was a very strange feeling for me. There was something almost symbolic about refusing the gift: I felt as if I would never see Carolyn again, and it wasn't a good feeling.

I went home and tried to undo the mess the bird had made, but I couldn't concentrate. I was overwhelmed by sadness. I tried to lie down and could barely function. One of my friends called, and it took all my energy to answer the phone. I told him I was feeling crushingly depressed, and he informed me that that was one of the side effects of ecstasy. "I wish I'd known that before I took it and fell in love with everyone," I said.

After I got off the phone, I realized that I had to get out of this horrible funk. I thought it might help if I went to the gym, so I dragged my sorry ass out of the apartment and into the street. When I reached Greenwich Avenue, I saw a school bus parked at the corner. There must have been thirty high-school girls milling around; they looked like part of a cheerleading squad. One of the girls saw me coming, did a double take, and then her face lit up.

"Hey!" she said. "You're that guy! You're the underwear guy!"

I didn't deny it. Pretty soon, I was surrounded by a bunch of screaming girls, jumping up and down and asking for my autograph. I must tell you: I loved it. It went a long way toward getting me out of my funk. I put in a good workout at the gym and walked home feeling a whole lot better. I was also marginally more clearheaded. I realized—again—that drugs and Michael Bergin weren't a good mix. I had to get my shit together.

One night, Tad came back to my apartment. He had been calling to apologize, and I finally got tired of hanging up on him. I'm also not big on holding grudges. So he came over to apologize in person, with a bottle of wine, and I accepted his apology. Then he got pushy. He wondered if I would take him back as my manager, and I told him, nicely, that that was never going to happen. I was still pretty steamed about the incident with the two doughy cops. As for that item in the gossip column about me and Valentino, well, I had my suspicions about Tad, but I honestly didn't feel like getting into it. What good would it have done either of us?

Suddenly, the buzzer rang. It was Carolyn. She needed to see me. It was an awkward situation. I told Tad he had to leave, that one of my friends was on her way up. He was very curious—"Who is she? Why can't I meet her? Why are you hiding her from me?"— but I finally got him out the door. Then I buzzed Carolyn and told her that Tad was on his way down, and that she should probably wait until he was out of sight. I was trying to protect her. She was seeing John Jr. at the time—already engaged to him, according to some of the tabloids—and I thought we should be discreet. I waited upstairs and Carolyn buzzed me again. She said she'd been out of sight, that Tad was gone, and would I please come down. She didn't feel like coming up.

She was waiting for me out front, with a baseball cap pulled low on her forehead. She said hi and I said hi, and we went over and sat on the stoop next door. She took my arm and began pinching it in that way she had. I noticed she was having a hard time looking me in the eye.

"What's the matter?" I asked. "You seem troubled."

"Nothing," she said, pinching away. She watched the passers-by for a while, engrossed.

"You sure you're okay?" I said.

"Yes," she said. "I just needed to see you."

It was very strange. She seemed uncomfortable in her own skin, fidgety, distant. And I wanted very much to help her. I know what you're thinking. As an outsider, as an unbiased observer, you probably think that Carolyn had treated me pretty shabbily. But I didn't see it that way. I still saw her as the generous, loving woman who had taken me under her wing when I first arrived in New York, the woman who had helped me find my way. And frankly, I was still in love with her.

"Let's walk," she said.

We only got as far as the pizzeria around the corner, on Sixth. We went in and I got two slices, but she didn't touch her food. She just sat across from me in the booth, holding on to my free arm, and worrying the skin between her fingers. I kept waiting for her to say something. I thought that she was actually there to talk to me about John Jr., to tell me that he had really proposed to her—that the tabloids had gotten it right for once—and that she had accepted. It was one of those things where you want to know but you don't want to know.

"Thanks for being here for me," she said, standing up.

"That's it?" I said. "Visit's over?"

She nodded and we went outside. She said she had to get back to her place, which wasn't far—she had a new apartment near Washington Square Park, though rumor had it that she was spending most of her time with John Jr. I offered to walk her home, but she shook her head sadly.

"No," she said. "I can't risk being seen with you." So she thanked me again, said good-bye, and hurried off.

A week later, she called me again. She said she needed to talk to me and invited me to her apartment. It was a nice place, a one-bedroom, larger than the studio. Some of the familiar things were there—the mattress, the empty picture frames—and the memories came flooding back.

I sat next to her on the bed, where we held hands and didn't say anything for a full minute.

"The reason I came to see you last week is that I was pregnant," she said. "I needed someone to talk to."

"You're having a baby?" I asked.

"No," she said. "I lost the baby. I had a miscarriage."

I spent the night with her. I knew it was wrong, and she knew it was wrong, but we both found ways to justify our behavior. She was probably thinking that she wasn't doing anything particularly duplicitous, since she hadn't yet committed to John Jr. But I don't know what she was thinking, frankly, because I didn't ask her, and she volunteered nothing. For my part, I was thinking that we might still end up together. After all, I was doing well now. I couldn't afford a compound, like the Kennedys, but I might one day be able to manage a little cottage on the beach.

After, as we drifted off to sleep, I began to think that maybe I still had a chance with her. I know it sounds crazy—it sounds crazy to me now, and it probably felt a little crazy even then—but it's a measure of how much I wanted her in my life. The way I saw it, she probably didn't even tell John Jr. about the pregnancy. She had come to me. What did that say about their relationship? And what did it say about ours?

We woke up at seven o'clock the following morning to someone pounding crazily at her door. I thought for sure it was John Jr., but it was Gordon. He was really worked up.

"Get the fuck out of here!" he told me. "He's on his way over."

Christ! John Jr. had been trying to reach Carolyn, but she had taken her phone off the hook when we went to bed. He hadn't been able to reach her, so he called Gordon to see if he knew where she was. When Gordon didn't have any news, John Jr. said he was going to ride over and make sure she was okay.

I looked at Carolyn—she was freaking—and booked the hell out of there. I ran off half dressed, with my shoes in my hand.

That was in April 1996.

The next time I saw Carolyn, she was a married woman.

7.

Mrs. John F. Kennedy Jr.

Nothing reopens the springs of love so fully as absence, and no absence so thoroughly as that which must needs be endless.
—Anthony Trollope, *The Last Chronicle of Barset*

In the weeks and months ahead, my only connection to Carolyn was through Gordon, and John Jr. wasn't wild about Gordon, so he didn't see much of her. When he did see her, however, he ragged on her about John Jr. Gordon thought Carolyn was making a big mistake. He told her over and over again that he thought she belonged with me.

Later that year, I took a small role in a Merchant-Ivory movie, *The Proprietor,* and between fashion shoots, I continued to audition for acting jobs. The casting people always had nice things to say, and I always left feeling wildly optimistic. But I would never hear from them again, and before long I realized that that is the nature of the movie business. People lie to you. Lies are so much easier than the truth.

Then the rumors started: Carolyn had accepted John Jr.'s proposal. They were getting married this week, next week, the week after next. I didn't believe it and kept my mind on my work. I was busy with a number of things, not the least of which was a Michael Bergin poster. I don't know how I got talked into that—it seems so egocentric—but the agency said it made sense, so I went along with the idea. After the shoot, the graphic artists went to work, and we decided to launch the poster on a Monday in late September.

But something else happened the day before the launch that took my mind off posters, work, and everything else. On September 21, 1996, I was alone in my apartment, doing crunches and half listening to the TV, when I heard the news. Carolyn Bessette and John F. Kennedy Jr. had tied the knot on Cumberland Island, a secluded little spit of land off the coast of Georgia. A small ceremony. Very tasteful. Forty people in a tiny, rundown church. The whole thing carefully scripted and choreographed to avoid the press. And of course no one could mention the event without pointing out how beautiful Carolyn had looked. She was glowing. A perfect princess for America's leading prince. To say I was stunned is an understatement. I felt nauseous. I stood and flipped through the channels to see what else I could learn, but the story was just breaking, and few people had details. I didn't know what to do with myself. My apartment suddenly felt horribly claustrophobic.

The last time I'd seen Carolyn was at her place: that morning when Gordon had arrived, warning us that John Jr. was on his way. I remember grabbing my things and running off like a coward. Suddenly I wondered if I should have stayed, if I should have held my ground. But it's not as if Carolyn had asked me to stay. Clearly the last thing she had wanted was a confrontation, but I probably should have made that decision on my own. If I had, maybe she'd have been marrying me, not him.

Gordon called me while I was reading an account of the ceremony in the *New York Times*. He was practically in tears. Carolyn had told him that he would design her wedding dress, if and when the day finally arrived, but instead she had gone to Narciso Rodriguez, an up-and-coming designer. Even worse, Gordon hadn't been invited to the wedding.

"I'll never forgive her," he said. But he said it without conviction. He'd already forgiven her. There was something about Carolyn that made it impossible to hate her.

I went out for a jog to clear my head and ran for the better part of an hour. I tried to make sense of what I was feeling, and it wasn't easy. On the one hand, I was crushed. I had known for some time now that Carolyn and John Jr. would probably end up together, but once in a while, selfishly, I found myself hoping that things wouldn't work out for them. Now that she'd gone through with it, however, I felt not only a terrible loss, but also an odd sense of relief. In a strange way, I'd been liberated. I could get on with my life. Of course I still loved Carolyn, and I genuinely wished her all the happiness in the world. But a little bitterness crept into the good wishes.

On Monday, I launched the official Michael Bergin poster at a midtown bar, and my old man came along for moral support. The media turned out in suspiciously large numbers—*ET* was there, so was *Hard Copy*, several local TV stations, and a dozen reporters, representing everyone from the *Post* to the *Daily News*—and I quickly found out why. The first question was, "How do you feel about your ex-girlfriend getting married over the weekend?" There were other questions, and all of them were about Carolyn and John Jr. Nobody asked about the poster. I smiled gamely and did what the heartbroken party usually does in cases like this: "Carolyn is a great person, and I wish her and John the very best." I meant what I said and felt good saying it.

After the failed launch, my father and I went to a nearby bar. There was a TV perched overhead, and at six-thirty *Hard Copy* came on with some footage of Carolyn and John Jr., along with a rehash of the little that was known about the wedding. Then my name came up, and there I was on the screen: the Other Man. There was a short commercial break—I guess I made a good cliff-hanger— followed by footage that had been shot at the underwhelming poster launch. I heard myself repeating almost verbatim what I'd said an hour earlier: "Carolyn is a terrific human being. John Jr. is a very lucky man. I hope they will be very happy together." Everyone in the bar had stopped to watch, and when it was over they burst into applause. I bowed my thanks, smiled sheepishly, and pretended I was unfazed. But I was fazed—trust me. Then we saw the same thing all over again, from *ET*'s point of view, and everyone clapped even louder. I smiled harder in response, then ordered another drink, a double. My father was the only person in the bar who could see how much I was hurting.

In the days and weeks ahead, you couldn't avoid Carolyn and John Jr. If you turned on the TV, there they were. If you walked past a newsstand, there they were in triplicate. I'd find myself on the subway reading about them in *People* magazine, over someone's shoulder. I was amazed by the way the press dissected it. Carolyn wasn't rich or famous or from some fancy family or a Hollywood starlet or a member of the European nobility. She was just a class act from a decent all-American family, and she was the epitome of class herself. John had chosen well, the pundits said. She was beautiful, stylish, smart, and charismatic. They went on at length about America's New Royal Couple carrying on the line, and from time to time there would be a sidebar on me, the Other Man, the one she didn't marry, *wisely*.

I got calls from reporters every day, sometimes three and four times a day.

"I have nothing to say," I repeated over and over again. "I think Carolyn is great, and I know she's going to be very happy." Some of the callers were quite persistent. Some mentioned large sums of money. I passed.

Eventually, they stopped hounding me, but Carolyn and John Jr. didn't get a break. There were stories about John Jr. asking the paparazzi to please give them a little privacy—it was so soon after their wedding—and more stories about how the paparazzi refused to heed his pleas. When Carolyn and John left their apartment to walk their dog, there were photographers there to record their every move. And if they caught Carolyn at an odd angle, an angle that suggested she might have gained a pound or two, there was endless speculation about a new Kennedy heir. I'm human. I read the stories, just like everyone else.

Before long, the tide began to turn. Now they were reporting that the honeymoon was over. Carolyn hated all the attention and the pressure of being Mrs. Kennedy, they said (and they always quoted "unnamed friends"). There were articles analyzing the meaning of celebrity, and how it affected certain people. I remember reading that John Jr. actually craved the attention, because he had lived in the spotlight all his life, and that his protestations were just part of a big act. His young wife, on the other hand, preferred to live in the shadows. She was a very private person, according to a source who had probably never met her. Another writer compared her to Jackie O., in both style and personality. He said she exhibited the same poise and grace as the late Mrs. Kennedy, and he made it sound as if John Jr. had married his mother.

Finally, the fascination with them abated, but only marginally. I don't think a week went by without some mention of them in the press. As for the photographs, they were everywhere. I found them hard to look at. Carolyn seemed so damn happy, he was so damn handsome, and they looked so damn good together—and so *rich*.

I wouldn't have noticed the money aspect, except that I was suddenly having serious financial problems. At one point, I had managed to amass close to a quarter of a million dollars, and I had entrusted it to a friend of mine at one of the major brokerage firms. He called me one dismal day to tell me that we had a problem: my account was down a bit. Well, not a bit: *a lot*. He'd made some bad calls on some big-name stocks, and I lost my shirt. I had approximately forty thousand dollars left to my name—less than 20 percent of my original investment. I couldn't believe it. So much of what I had worked for up until that day—gone.

For the better part of a week, I lay in bed like a catatonic. I only moved when the guy from the deli showed up with another delivery. Then I decided to pull myself together. I called my agency and said I needed work.

I got a few gigs, went home for Christmas, then came back to the city and got more jobs. It was uninspiring work, always more of the same—"bend over, look pouty, let's see those abs"—but it was money.

After I did a campaign for Valentino, he called from Rome to ask me how it had gone and how I was doing. He knew about Carolyn—we'd already talked about her at length—and I told him I was learning to live without her. As for the shoot, it had gone very well. But me, personally? Well, I'd just lost most of my money, and I told him about that fateful call from my friend, the broker. When I was done, he asked me to give him the name of my bank and account number.

"What for?" I said.

"Just give me the number," he barked in his Italian accent. "And check with your bank tomorrow."

The following day, Valentino wired twenty thousand dollars into my account. When I called to tell him I couldn't accept it, he told me not to be a fool. Then I said I'd take it, because I needed it, but that I considered it a loan, and that I would repay him as soon as I had the funds. "Don't be reedeeculous," he said. "You are like a son to me."

In February 1997, VH-1 flew me to Puerto Vallarta, Mexico, for a special on sex appeal. My cohost was Daniela Pestova, the Victoria's Secret model who had recently graced the pages of *Sports Illustrated*. Toward the end of the shoot, I got a call from L.A. asking if

I'd be interested in auditioning for *Baywatch*. I thought the audition went horribly—I wanted the part, and I was pretty nervous—but when I landed back in New York and checked my messages, I heard the good news on my answering machine: the part was mine. I went crazy. I ran through the airport terminal shouting, "I got the part! I got the part!" People were staring at me like I was nuts, which I was, but it didn't stop me. "I got the part!" I hollered, running out into the bitter cold in nothing but a T-shirt. "Look at me, I'm John Travolta!"

The job didn't start until June, so I stuck around the East Coast for a couple of parties. One was my father's retirement party, back in Naugatuck. He was leaving the state police and joining Travelers Insurance as a private investigator. I felt as if I were retiring too: I was leaving modeling and beginning a new life as an actor.

Next was Gordon's birthday party, which took place in Manhattan, at a restaurant called Independent. He had invited Carolyn of course, but he really didn't think she would show up. There were about a dozen of us there, including Bill Cosby's daughter Erika, and we were hanging out drinking when Carolyn arrived. She saw me and nodded hello, and went over to kiss Gordon on the cheek. She didn't approach me, nor I her. It was a little awkward. Everyone knew our history.

Midway through the evening, Erika invited us to her father's place. We left the club and took three different cabs. I thought maybe I'd get lucky and ride up with Carolyn, but it didn't work out that way.

Erika led the way into her father's brownstone. The smell of flowers hit me before I had even stepped into the foyer, and as soon as I came through I saw that the whole place was ablaze with white carnations. There was something a little eerie about it, and then Erika explained that they were for her brother, Ennis. Suddenly I remembered the story: Ennis Cosby had been shot and killed in Los

Angeles the previous January while changing a tire at a freeway off-ramp. Erika took us to Ennis's room and began telling stories about him, and pretty soon she had half the place in tears. I left and went downstairs to get a drink and found Carolyn in the kitchen. She was with Gordon, but when I stepped through, Gordon had the good sense to leave. I looked at her and she looked at me, and neither of us said a word for what seemed like an entire minute.

"Meow," she said finally.

"Meow," I replied.

It was hard for both of us. She had trouble meeting my eyes.

"Congratulations on your marriage," I said, and she looked up to see if I meant it. I *did* mean it, and she could tell.

"Thank you," she said. "Congratulations on *Baywatch*."

"Thanks," I said.

"Gordon told me the good news," she said.

There was another awkward pause. I couldn't get over how beautiful she looked.

"I am genuinely happy for you, Carolyn. I mean that, from the bottom of my heart. And I want you to be happy. You deserve it."

Then a guy came in with a hand mirror and a vial of cocaine, and began chopping lines, right there at the marble counter. He offered the mirror to Carolyn. She smiled politely and said, "No, thanks." Then he offered it to me and I also demurred. He did all four lines himself.

I looked at Carolyn. There was so much more I wanted to say, but our moment of privacy had come and gone. I didn't talk to her again for the rest of the evening, and the next time I heard from her I was living in L.A.

I moved to Los Angeles in April, a few weeks after Gordon's birthday party. I found a two-bedroom place on Laurel Avenue, near Sunset, and got busy trying to furnish it. The money Valentino had sent me came in very handy, as did the news that Claiborne wanted to sign me to a two-year contract. The Claiborne contract paid six hundred thousand dollars, which was very comforting indeed: that first year out with *Baywatch* my salary was only thirty thousand dollars.

I wasn't going to start work on the series until June, so I had plenty of time to get to know Los Angeles, and I was still happy to take modeling jobs.

My phone rang early one morning. It was Carolyn. She had been wanting to call to say good-bye and wish me luck but had put it off too long and now I was gone.

"I got your number from Gordon," she told me, and I could hear the longing in her voice. "I hope you don't mind I'm calling now."

"I don't mind at all," I said.

"How's it going?"

"I don't know yet," I said. "Good, I think. I'm just settling in. I like my new place, and I'm finding my way around. What about you?"

"I'm fine," she said. *Fine*. Typical laconic Carolyn. "When will I see you again?"

"Funny you should ask," I said. "I actually have to fly back to New York next week for a runway show."

"Will you let me know when you're coming?" she asked.

"I sure will," I said.

The next day, on April 29, 1997, I got a call about a story in the *Star*. I rushed out to buy it. JFK JR. FURY AS BRIDE'S CAUGHT WITH BAYWATCH HUNK. I couldn't believe it. The article suggested that Carolyn was pissed at John Jr. for having snuck off to see his old flame Daryl, and that she was paying him back. It reported that Carolyn and I were secretly seeing each other and "burning up the phone lines" between New York and L.A. The story went into some detail about our "sizzling relationship," then stated that I had offered Carolyn a guest spot on *Baywatch*. I hadn't even started work on the series yet, but why let reality get in the way of a good story? The crux of the article was that the marriage was in serious trouble, and the capper was that Carolyn was pregnant.

I called Gordon to see what was up, but he didn't know much. Either that or he knew everything and was too discreet to share. Still, he read the same trash and heard the same rumors: That the marriage really was in trouble. That Carolyn was unhappy. That she felt she had made a mistake.

"I told her she was making a mistake," he added. "But she didn't listen."

"She looked great at your birthday party," I said.

"Looks are deceiving," he said.

As soon as I hung up, the phone rang. It was Valentino, calling from Rome. He was very worked up. "What ees wrong with you?" he sputtered. "Are you fuckeeng crazy? This is the Kennedys! The most powerful family in America. They will disappear you like they disappeared Marilyn Monroe!"

"None of it is true!" I protested.

"You stay away from that girl!" he said. "You hear me?"

I didn't hear him. When I went back to New York for my runway show—four hours of work for eighteen thousand dollars—Carolyn came to see me at the Marriott. She looked stunning, and I told her so.

"Thank you," she said.

I wanted to ask her about the rumors, but I knew better. Still, it was very strange having Carolyn standing there, in my hotel room, at a safe distance. We hadn't even given each other a kiss hello. I guess we both thought it probably wasn't a good idea.

"I brought you something," she said. She handed me a little box. There was a St. Christopher medal on a gold chain inside, and she had etched an X and an O onto the back with a safety pin. "Hugs and kisses," she explained. "From me."

"That's very sweet," I said.

"St. Christopher," she said. "You know, for protection. Because I'm not around to protect you anymore."

I couldn't hold back. I reached for her hand and pulled her to the bed. We kissed, but suddenly Carolyn pulled away.

"No," she said. "We can't." She didn't want to be weak. She kissed me on the cheek and hurried away.

The next day, missing her more than ever and feeling guilty for having been so weak, I was on a plane back to Los Angeles.

8.

Baywatch

Pains of love be sweeter far
Than all other pleasures are.
—John Dryden, *Tyrannic Love*

In June 1997, I was on the beach in Santa Monica with the cast and crew of *Baywatch* for my first day of shooting. I didn't have much experience with television, and I was nervous. Plus, I couldn't believe this was really happening to me. I'd be in the middle of a scene, and I'd start thinking "Oh my God, I'm on *Baywatch*!" It was nerve-racking and exciting and more than a little strange. Here I was, playing Jack "J.D." Darius, a lifeguard. If you couldn't figure it out by watching me run across the sand, you had the skimpy Speedos to remind you: the word "Baywatch" was written across my ass.

Within days, I was in the swing of it. I was an *actor*. I didn't think Laurence Olivier had anything to worry about, but then again, he probably hadn't started with Shakespeare either. Or had he?

The people on *Baywatch* were about as nice a group of people as I had ever worked with. And the women were unreal (in more ways than what met the eye). I made some good friends on the set, but I was lonely and wanted more. One night I got home to a cryptic message from Carolyn. She asked me to please call her the next day at work.

I reached her early the next morning.

"How much room do you have in your apartment?" she asked.

"Plenty," I said. "Why?"

"Gordon and I are coming out."

She wasn't kidding. In late June or early July, she and Gordon came to L.A. I couldn't pick them up at the airport—within the past year, Carolyn had become one of the most photographed women in America, and we couldn't risk being seen—so they took a cab to my place. When I heard them pull up, I rushed out to meet them. Carolyn was already out of the cab, and she was almost unrecognizable. She had a baseball cap pulled low on her forehead and wore dark sunglasses.

"Hey," she said, and smiled. Her whole face lit up.

"Hey," I said back.

We hugged each other and she gave me a chaste little kiss on the cheek.

We ordered in that night and right away it felt like old times. It felt, in fact, like that period when Carolyn and I had redefined our relationship, when we had gone from being lovers to being friends. Of course it was a little confusing. I didn't know what Carolyn was doing there, and I was afraid to ask.

Still, I was very happy to have her, and she seemed very happy to be there. I quickly forgot that she was married.

We crashed early because they were tired from the trip and still on New York time. Carolyn slept in the second bedroom, and Gordon took the couch. I left for work before they were up, and they were waiting for me when I got home. Carolyn forgot herself for a moment and threw her arms around my neck and gave me a big kiss on the lips. We had dinner, watched a video, and all went back to our respective beds. That night, I lay in my room and thought about Carolyn. I wondered if she was thinking about me.

On the third night, Carolyn and I realized we weren't going to be able to resist each other—the flesh was weak—and she ended up in my bed. I killed the lights and we got under the covers. I was as nervous as a virgin.

"We shouldn't be doing this, should we?" I said.

"I think John's having an affair," she said.

"Why would you think that?"

"I don't know," she said. "I just do."

John was apparently off in Iceland, kayaking with a group of friends. He would be gone for at least two weeks. Had Carolyn told him she was leaving town? And if so, where had she said she was going? I thought the whole thing was pretty odd. What if he called? They had phones in Iceland, right? You don't leave your wife for two weeks and not talk to her. Or maybe you do. If you're having problems. Maybe Carolyn and John had agreed to take some time off from each other. Maybe the tabloids had it right after all.

It was also possible that John Jr. really *was* having an affair, as Carolyn suspected. On the other hand, maybe Carolyn was only trying to justify her own behavior.

But suddenly none of that mattered; suddenly we were making love. Carolyn and I were locked in each other's arms, and it was everything I remembered it to be and more. It brought back all the craziness. All the subterfuge and lying and madness and abuse, all the things you put up with when you're in love. And I was in love all over again. I knew this was wrong, but my emotions already had the better of me, and emotions don't leave much room for logic.

For the next three days, I'd run off early to work and leave Gordon and Carolyn to their own devices. At the end of the day, I'd come back to the apartment to find them waiting for me. They'd gone to the beach or for a walk or shopping for dinner. There would be a bottle of wine on the table, along with a nice Brie, already at room temperature, and a little something in the oven. It felt weirdly homey. I would look at Carolyn and think, *This is what it could have been like for us. This is how it should have turned out.*

On Friday, with the weekend looming, Gordon went back to New York. Carolyn had told him that she wanted to be alone with me. For the next few nights, it was just the two of us. I felt like we were in the middle of an old-fashioned TV series about an idioti-cally happy couple. Here I was, coming home to my lovely wife, who always lit up when I walked through the door. All we needed now were a few kids. But then I'd remember: *She's not my wife. She's married to someone else. She chose him over me.*

We didn't talk about this, of course. How could we? To talk about John Jr. and Carolyn's marriage and her new life in the public eye would only have served to show us how insane we were.

During the day that weekend, we went out, with Carolyn in her loose-fitting corduroys and a baseball cap, pulled low on her fore-head, right up against her dark glasses. She didn't want to risk being recognized. We walked along Third Street, went into stores, and window-shopped like we used to do in SoHo.

One day, she bought me a huge vase and filled it with tall dried flowers. Then she bought a second vase for the living room and dec-orative pillows for my couch. A small painting. A metal garbage pail for the kitchen. I'd look at her and think, *She's behaving like a wife.*

At night, we'd order in or I'd run around the corner for sushi. We'd feed each other. We'd make love. And everything remained unsaid. It was killing me, and I imagined it must have been killing her too.

On the last day, the day of her flight home, we got out of bed late and I had to hurry off to work. She was planning to take a cab to the airport. I asked her if she had money. She nodded. I kissed her and thanked her for coming and told her how nice it had been to see her again. She told me it had been nice to see me too, and she walked me to the door and kissed me good-bye. It all seemed strangely sedate. I don't know what I'd been expecting. More emotion, maybe?

When I got home, she was waiting for me on the stoop. She threw her arms around me and told me she was sorry but she couldn't leave me. Now I got all the emotion that had been missing that morning. Almost more than I could handle. She was married, for God's sake. What were we doing? What were we thinking?

The next day, we piled into my Jeep and I drove her to the airport. I wanted to tell her that I loved her, but I couldn't do it. It wouldn't have been fair to her, but I wasn't only thinking about her. I was thinking about me too. I really did love her. But she'd made up her mind, and there was no turning back. What was the point of all this torture?

When we reached the airport, I dropped her at the curb, discreetly, and watched her hurry off. I raced away, already late for work, and tried not to think about her. But I already missed her horribly. I felt like there was a huge hole inside me.

That night, I got back to the apartment and saw that she had left her perfume on my night table. Egyptian Musk. I loved the way it smelled. For weeks afterward, I would put a little dab of it on my wrist after my morning shower. I wanted to have her with me throughout the day.

It was crazy. I was torturing myself, and I knew it. Plus, now I began to feel horribly guilty about the whole experience. One morning, I tossed the perfume. I also wanted to toss the black sweatpants she'd left behind, but I couldn't bring myself to do it.

I made a concerted effort not to think about her. I really did. But sometimes I couldn't avoid her even when I tried: the newspapers and magazines were always in my face. I remember reading that John Jr. had cut a serious gash in his right wrist while clearing the dishes at home. I thought that sounded a little suspect. I also read that he was becoming a pretty respected publisher, and I actually went out and bought a copy of his magazine, *George*. There was an article in one of the issues that he had written himself. The only thing I remember about it was a description of his cousins Joseph and Michael as "poster boys for bad behavior."

I spoke to Gordon one day, to see what was going on. He said he didn't know much because he hadn't seen Carolyn at all in recent weeks. Maybe she and John Jr. weren't fighting as much as they used to, he said. Then again, he'd heard that the magazine was taking over John Jr.'s life, and that he was going to use it as a stepping stone into politics. I wondered how Carolyn felt about this. Maybe it was a good thing he was busy: you escape into your work and your problems recede into the background.

I was busy with my work too of course. And it was good for me. Carolyn was back in New York. With her husband. Getting on with her life. I would get on with mine.

I became friendly with one of the stars of the show. One night we had a few tequilas and ended up in bed. That same week, one of the featured regulars told me she was looking for an apartment, and I told her she could move into mine. It wasn't my intention to sleep with her, but I did. And she had an ex-boyfriend back east who got pretty upset. I'd already had some experience with boyfriends and ex-boyfriends. Remember the exotic dancer and the threat of "serious damage"? I hoped this wasn't more of the same.

It was a very odd time for me. My professional life was going great. My personal life, however, was another story. People look at me and make all sorts of assumptions about the type of man I am, but at heart I'm a complete romantic. I'm not into flings; I'm into love.

In September, as I struggled to make sense of my personal life, Carolyn called to say she missed me too much and couldn't stay away.

"I need to see you again," she said.

"What are you going to tell John?" I asked.

"I've already told him," she said. "I said I was going out to visit a girlfriend."

So it was done. She had already decided.

I couldn't put her up at my place, since I had a roommate, and we couldn't risk anyone finding out about us, so she took a room at a downscale Days Inn on Sunset Boulevard.

I was at work when her plane landed so I couldn't pick her up at the airport, but when I went to see her at the hotel she lit up the way she always used to. We embraced like long-lost lovers, ordered Thai takeout, and once again tried not to broach any subject that might put a damper on our good mood. It didn't work. By midnight, she looked confused and unhappy. I tried to get her to open up, but she didn't feel like talking. She asked me to lie next to her on the bed, and she worried the skin on my forearm like she used to. She didn't say anything. She seemed lost deep inside herself. And I didn't say much either. I really didn't need to ask her what was wrong. I knew what was wrong. She was having an affair. People don't have affairs unless they're unhappy in their marriages.

Unfortunately, I didn't have as much time for her as she had hoped. I was very busy with the series, and I was involved, or half involved, with my roommate. Maybe I could have made more time, but I think part of me—the *wiser* part of me—was trying to distance myself from Carolyn. It's not that I loved her less, but I wanted to love her less. I knew this relationship wasn't going anywhere, and I suspected it wouldn't end well.

She must have sensed my distance. When she left, she was more unhappy than ever. Oddly enough, I thought this was a step in the right direction.

9.

Things Fall Apart

Ever has it been that love knows not its own depth until the hour of separation.
—Kahlil Gibran

Thanksgiving came around, and I flew home to see my family. The Friday after the big meal, the phone rang. My father answered.

"Hello," a woman said. "Is Michael there? It's Mary."

My father handed me the phone. "It's 'Mary,'" he said, and gave me an odd look. I wondered if he knew.

It was Carolyn, of course. She asked if she could see me. We met at a seedy motel in nearby Milford that evening. She showed up behind the wheel of a Range Rover. I got us a room, and we went inside and made love without saying much. It felt wrong, but I guess morality wasn't much on our minds. It felt as if we were in one of those noir movies from the 1950s: the married woman and the amoral cad, lying in bed in a cheap motel room, with the neon light blinking outside.

In the early morning, we got dressed and left the room. She kissed me and got into her Range Rover and drove away. We hadn't said more than a couple dozen words to each other. I went back to Naugatuck, wondering what the hell it all meant. I was confused and needed help figuring things out. I wanted someone to talk to. But who could I talk to? I was sleeping with John F. Kennedy Jr.'s wife.

I started a journal. I was trying to make sense of my relationship with Carolyn because it was eating away at me. I needed to get it out. I needed to deal with it. She was somebody else's wife, for God's sake, and I still loved her. And until I got her out of my system I wasn't going to be able to move on. I knew that it was over, but there's knowing and there's *knowing*. I still wasn't free of her. Nor her of me.

Shortly before Christmas, I went to New York and landed a guest spot on *The Cosby Show*. I played a good-looking klutz who couldn't do anything right. I also had a dream sequence where I made out with Madeline Kahn. It was a welcome distraction from my real life. I had never done physical comedy, and it was fun. I remember during rehearsals, I was sweeping away with a broom when Bill Cosby stopped me and asked me to do it a different way. He showed me how he wanted it done, and I told him that I thought it worked better the other way. Suddenly, the whole set went dead silent. Everyone was frozen, not breathing. I think they expected Cosby to explode or something, but he didn't explode. Still, I rethought my position and decided to sweep the floor his way after all.

The distraction didn't last. Carolyn tracked me down while I was still in the city. Gordon told her that I was staying near Lincoln Center and she insisted on coming over. She had something for me, she said. She'd only stay a minute. Promise. She showed up at the hotel, looking as beautiful as ever, but skittish. There was something a little manic in her eyes. She gave me a beautiful gold lighter with my initials engraved across one side. I didn't have anything for her and told her I felt lousy about it.

"Don't be silly," she said. "Just seeing you is more than enough." Then she kissed me on the cheek and hurried off.

I thought, *Okay. Good. Nothing happened. We are getting through this. It's over. We are going to get on with our respective lives.*

I spent Christmas with my family and went back to L.A. for the New Year, feeling marginally more optimistic about moving on, about managing life without Carolyn.

But there was more unrest around the corner. My roommate's boyfriend took to calling the apartment at all hours of the day and night. Whenever I answered, he'd threaten to come to L.A. and kick my ass. I told him he was crazy, that nothing was going on between me and his so-called girlfriend, and I warned him that I'd call the cops if he kept bothering me. It didn't help. It became something of a nightmare. I began to avoid my roommate and felt as if I was caught in the middle of a triangle. I knew from personal experience that triangles are never easy. I'd been in one for a long time. And it seemed I was in it still. What the hell was wrong with me?

In the spring of 1998, Gordon's mother passed away. He called with the sad news and asked if I'd meet him in Seattle for the service. "Carolyn is coming with me," he said.

I flew up that Friday and met them at the airport. I hugged Gordon first—he looked like hell; he'd been very close to his mother—then hugged Carolyn. It struck me that the last time I saw the two of them, at the airport in Los Angeles, I had hugged Carolyn first.

Carolyn saw that I was wearing the St. Christopher's medal she'd given me. She flipped it over and noticed that the X and the O she'd etched on the back had faded a little.

"I'll fix that for you," she said.

We left the terminal and took a cab to a little bed-and-breakfast that was holding two rooms for us. There was a door between the two rooms, one of which had two beds. Carolyn didn't say anything. She just looked at me, and it was understood that she and I were going to take the room with two beds.

Gordon glanced at his watch. Some of his friends and relatives were waiting for us at a downtown bar, and he was eager to go. He wanted to get drunk to numb the pain. We went and met his friends. Gordon and I both had a bit too much to drink, but Carolyn nursed one glass of wine all night.

We got back late, and Carolyn and I slipped into bed and made love. We were always tender with each other, but on this particular night she was unusually tender, as if I were so delicate that I might break under her touch. I felt so in love with her I thought I would burst, and it killed me.

The next day, we went to the service at a small chapel, then over to the house where Gordon's mother had lived out her final years. There was a small party, and when everybody left we helped Gordon sift through some of his mother's belongings. We looked at photo albums of the family and at pictures of Gordon growing up. He got sad all over again and decided he wanted to go drinking, so once again we hooked up with some friends of his and hit the bars.

About an hour into it, Carolyn wanted to leave, and she wanted me to go with her. We got back to our room and made love again. We fell asleep, clinging to each other. Hours later, I heard Gordon stumbling up the stairs and into bed.

In the morning, Carolyn seemed very lethargic. "You look unhappy," I said. "What can I do?"

"Save me," she said.

I smiled at her, as if she had said this to amuse me, but she didn't smile back. We had breakfast and returned to the room. Gordon was just waking up. He said he had to go over to his mother's house again for a little while. "When I get back," he added, "we'll get ready for Fresno."

"Fresno?"

"Did I forget to tell you?" he said. "We're burying her in Fresno."

"I wish I'd known that earlier," I said. "I have a round-trip ticket, and I can't change it."

I didn't want to go to Fresno, frankly. I'd come to be there for Gordon in his time of need, and I'd also come to see Carolyn. I'd be lying if I said otherwise, but a third leg of the trip seemed out of the question. Carolyn was very upset.

"You have to come to Fresno," she insisted after Gordon left. She reached for the phone to call the airlines. "Give me your ticket. I'll change it. I'll pay for it."

"I can't," I said. "I have to get back to L.A. for a guest spot on *Access Hollywood*."

"When?"

"Tomorrow," I said. "Monday."

"Cancel it," she said.

"Not possible," I said. "It's locked, and I need this gig."

Carolyn looked like she was near panic, but I held firm. I decided to sweat some of the alcohol out of my system, so I put on my running shoes and went for a jog. When I came back from my run, I asked the young girl at the front desk if she could call me a cab in about an hour and went upstairs. Carolyn was lying in bed, propped up on the pillows, waiting for me. She looked gaunt and withdrawn—ill, in fact.

"You okay?" I asked.

"What do you think?" she said.

It was spooky. I got in the shower, then dressed, and began to pack my bags. She watched.

"I looked in your things," she said. I turned to face her. "I looked in your book and it's not true. *Access Hollywood* isn't until Tuesday. You lied to me. You could come to Fresno if you wanted. Why did you lie to me?"

I didn't answer. She started to cry.

"Don't you understand?" she said. "I love you. I want to be with you."

"Carolyn," I said. "Don't say that. You know it's not true. You're just upset."

"But it is," she insisted, crying harder. She was getting hysterical. "I can't go on. I don't want to go on."

"Stop," I said.

"Please, Michael—please forgive me."

"For what?" I said.

She began to bawl uncontrollably, huge, gasping sobs, so powerful she could hardly catch her breath.

"For the way I've hurt you," she said. "I know how much I've hurt you. But you have to help me, Michael. We have to do this."

We? Jesus. Suddenly it was *we?*

"We're not doing anything, Carolyn," I said.

I was getting scared. I was watching her come apart at the seams, and I didn't know what to do. I had always been there for Carolyn. If she called because she needed to talk, I listened. If she wanted me for one night, I went. If she needed company at a family party, I was there. And if she wanted to get together in a seedy motel room, I got in my car and met her, even when it went against my better judgment. But this was different. She was asking for something I couldn't deliver and didn't want to deliver. She was asking me to give her the strength to leave her husband.

"I don't think you're thinking clearly," I said. "I don't think you've thought this through."

"Don't say that!" she shouted. "I've thought about nothing else." She seemed on the verge of physical and mental collapse. "I love you! I want to be with you!"

Now I was terrified. I was actually shaking. I couldn't even begin to process what she was asking of me.

"Carolyn," I said. "Pull yourself together. This isn't about me. This is about you. This is a problem I can't fix."

"But it *is* about you!" she protested. "We can do this."

"Look," I said, raising my hands in surrender. "I love you, and I've always loved you, but if you think you're just going to get up and walk out on him, you're not thinking very clearly. This is not the type of scandal that people forget. This will follow us around for the rest of our lives."

"Who cares?" she said. "Who cares about a lousy scandal?"

"I do," I said. I couldn't believe she was ready to get out of her marriage. I couldn't believe *she* believed it. "I don't want a scandal and I don't want the responsibility for a scandal. It will be way bigger than you can imagine."

My words seemed to be coming from someone else's mouth. I loved Carolyn, and over the years I had shown—sometimes to my detriment—that I would do anything for her. But this was too much. I was unwilling to be part of this.

"Please, Michael!" she begged. She was frantically worrying the skin on her own arm.

"No," I said.

That was my last word to Carolyn. *No.* I grabbed my bag and went downstairs. The cab was already there, thankfully, and I hopped in and told the driver to take off. As he pulled away, Carolyn came running outside. She called out to me, but I didn't want to deal with it anymore.

"Just go," I told the driver, and he pulled away.

"Michael!"

I turned around. She had drifted out into the middle of the street, and she was looking right at me, growing smaller and smaller. Her head was tilted slightly to the left, and her arms were hanging limply at her sides. She looked as if she barely had the energy to hold herself up. Then the cab turned the corner, and she disappeared from view.

I slept badly Sunday night. I couldn't stop thinking about her. I called her cell phone late Monday, expecting that she'd be back in New York, but I got voice mail. I left a message: "Worried about you. Please call." She didn't call. I tried again the next day, and again she didn't call.

I tried to tell myself that I had done the right thing, but it didn't make me feel any better.

On Tuesday I contacted *Access Hollywood* to confirm the time. I was cohosting a segment on fashion, and I had to get ready. I mentioned that I needed a haircut, and I was sent off to see the show's best stylist. Her name was Joy Tilk. She was smart, funny, and gorgeous, and I felt better just listening to her. She also did a great job cutting my hair, so I asked if I might call her for regular haircuts. She said sure and gave me her home number.

I did my segment, went home, and tried to forget the weekend in Seattle. I got back into the swing of things. Reading scripts. Running to the gym for a game of basketball. Working out at Billy Blank's studio. Anything to get my mind off Carolyn. I also had my duties on *Baywatch*: swimming, battling waves, jumping off piers. Being busy helped, as always.

One afternoon, I got out of the shower and looked at myself in the mirror. I didn't need a haircut, but I called Joy anyway. I went over to her place and she trimmed my hair. I was shy about offering her money, so I asked if I could take her out. On Friday, I picked her up and we went to see *Ever After*, with Drew Barrymore. Then we went to dinner at Lola's, a restaurant on Fairfax, near Melrose, owned by a friend of mine. We had a couple of margaritas with dinner and a couple more after dinner, and then we went back to her house. We ended up spending the whole weekend together.

Late Sunday, I took her to a friend's party. It was nice. In fact, I was surprised at how nice it was. I felt good around her, and I think it scared me a little. I knew I wasn't over Carolyn and I didn't think I wanted to jump into another relationship. I didn't think it was healthy. I had to pull myself together first, emotionally speaking. Still, there was something about Joy that was hard to resist. And she made it easy. There was no pressure. No questions. We got together when we wanted to get together, and we found ourselves getting together more and more.

This went on for several months. We were together but not together. I didn't call her my girlfriend, since I'd learned from Carolyn that labels are unnecessary, and Joy never pressured me.

I went home for Thanksgiving and stayed all the way through Christmas. I had a great time with my family, as always, and it was made all the better when my sister told us she was pregnant. I was going to be an uncle for the first time. I found myself getting very emotional about it. I love kids. I have always loved them. I believe it dates back to when I was a kid myself, taking care of my little sister. I have always wanted a big family—a family like mine—and suddenly I couldn't get the idea of family out of my head. I thought about it all the way back to L.A.; I thought about the fact that I was going to be thirty years old and that I should probably have kids soon, while I was still young enough to enjoy them.

Back home, just in from the airport, I called Joy. I had missed her, and I couldn't understand why she sounded so terse on the phone. I asked her to come over. She walked in and right away I could see that she was seriously pissed. I'd been gone for several weeks, and I hadn't called her. It reminded me of Milan, of the way I'd messed up by not calling Carolyn, and I realized I'd just done it again. I was a fuckup, no question. I also realized something else: for all of Joy's talk about a relationship with no strings and no expectations, it was clear she had expectations after all.

I still didn't think I was ready for this. We argued, then we made love, and then we argued some more. She walked out in tears and suddenly it was over. I felt lousy about it. I really liked Joy. I didn't want to lose her, but I didn't know how to keep her in my life without making more of a commitment, and I wasn't ready for a commitment. I was still damaged from my years with Carolyn.

Three weeks later, the phone rang. It was Joy.

"I'm pregnant," she said.

Jesus. What next?

I drove over to see her. I was pretty freaked out, as you can probably imagine. On the other hand, I'd been feeling the pull of fatherhood since my visit home, and I was still feeling it. I wondered if God was trying to tell me something.

By the time I pulled up at her place, I was seriously confused. Even if God *was* trying to tell me something, was I really ready for this? I didn't think so. In fact, as I walked though Joy's front door I had managed to convince myself that I wouldn't be ready for children for a good many years, if ever, and that I wasn't ready for this responsibility. And that's what I told Joy. I said it harshly and in no uncertain terms.

Joy stood her ground. She didn't believe in abortion. She was going to have the baby. I felt scared and cornered, and I behaved like a major asshole. I told her, "If you want to have this kid, go ahead and have it. But don't look at me. You're going to be a single mother, and I'm going to be a single father." Then I stormed out of the house.

Joy called me and tried to reason with me, but I didn't want to listen. The truth is, I was terrified. I had loved Carolyn in a passionate, obsessive way, and I had been badly hurt. I didn't want to be hurt again. I cared for Joy deeply, but I'd put up a wall between us. I was intent on protecting myself. I'd had enough pain in my life.

It got ugly. We were fighting over a child that hadn't been born yet, a child neither of us had met. It was madness. There was a life growing inside her, and it belonged to both of us, and we were acting like a couple of crazy people.

After several weeks of this insanity, I broke down and called her to apologize. I asked her to give me a chance to undo the shitty things I'd said and done, and told her I wanted to be the best father I could be. "Where can I begin?" I asked.

The following week, we went for the ultrasound together, and Christ if that didn't get me in the gut. To see this little person in there, glowing, moving, looking like he was waving hello, touched parts of me I hadn't known existed. Suddenly I was excited and optimistic. I was getting on with my life. I was going to have a family. Things weren't perfect between Joy and me, no, but we were going to make them work.

That May, in 1999, Gordon came out to visit a friend of his, the sister-in-law of Reggie Miller, of the Indiana Pacers. Reggie had a big house in the Hollywood Hills, and I went over and hooked up with Gordon and stayed for drinks and a barbecue. Before long, inevitably, we were talking about Carolyn. There were rumors that she and John Jr. had hit a very rough patch. Gordon had heard that they fought constantly and that John Jr. had actually moved out of the loft at one point, but it was just the usual bullshit. People can't seem to get enough of other people's misery, I guess. It must make them feel better about their own crazy lives.

I told Gordon about Joy, and about some of the rocky times we had gone through ourselves, and were in fact *still* going through. And I told him we were struggling to make sense of things.

"It's very important to me," I said. "Especially now that she's pregnant."

"Pregnant?!" Gordon lit up. "I can't believe it," he said, grinning ear to ear. "Michael's going be a daddy!"

"I can't believe it either," I said, and I was grinning too.

A few weeks later, in June, I flew to Honolulu for my first week on *Baywatch Hawaii*. I came back to L.A. every second or third weekend to see Joy. The reality began to sink in. I was going to try to make a life with this woman. I was going to be a *father*.

On Friday, July 16, I had a late shoot and went to bed late. The following morning, I got up, brushed my teeth, turned on my cell phone, and realized that dozens of people had been trying to call me. Before I could check my voice mail, the phone rang again. It was Joy, calling from Los Angeles. Had I heard the news? JFK Jr.'s plane had been reported missing the night before. Carolyn and her sister Lauren had been on board with him. They had left Fairfield, New Jersey, en route to Martha's Vineyard. The plan had been to drop Lauren at Martha's Vineyard, then continue to Hyannis Port, Massachusetts, to attend the wedding of Rory Kennedy, the youngest daughter of the late Bobby Kennedy.

They never made it.

I didn't want to believe it. My thought was the plane is *missing*. It'll turn up, right? They'll be okay, right?

I turned on the news. The Coast Guard was out in full force, and the media were still referring to it as a search-and-rescue operation. I called Carolyn's mother, in Connecticut, and told her not to give up hope. But even as we spoke, the news turned grim. Searchers had found pieces of the plane, along with some personal items. They weren't holding out much hope. From one moment to the next, search-and-rescue had become search-and-recovery.

My phone kept ringing. A woman at the *Baywatch* production office said reporters had been calling from around the world. They were looking for a reaction from the ex-boyfriend. I didn't have anything to say to the press. I called Carolyn's mother again. When I heard her voice, I began to sob. I had called to comfort her, and instead she was comforting me.

"You were very special to her, Michael," she said. "We will keep her in our hearts forever."

I showed up for work, late. Everyone knew about my relationship with Carolyn, and many of them were staring at me as if they wanted to say something but didn't know where to begin. What do you say to the other man? What role does he have in this, if any?

People called throughout the day. Joy. Family. Friends. More reporters. I got through to Gordon, in New York, who was numb. He simply didn't want to believe it.

Toward the end of the day, one of the men on the production crew, a big ruddy-faced Hawaiian, took me aside and told me what he'd done when his father passed away a few years earlier. He'd paddled out to sea at sunset, with a lei of fresh flowers, and said a final prayer. As he prayed, he had torn the flowers off, one at a time, and left a trail of them on the surface of the water. When he was finished, he turned and paddled back to shore.

The next day, I bought a beautiful lei in the lobby of the hotel. I borrowed a surfboard, paddled out to sea at sunset, and said goodbye to Carolyn. Then I turned around and paddled back in darkness, toward the glittering lights on the distant shore.

The next day, I received an invitation to the memorial service from Carolyn's mother. But I knew I couldn't go. I couldn't do that to her, the family, or the Kennedys. And I certainly didn't want to face the press.

The stories about John Jr. and Carolyn kept coming. A *torrent* of stories. You couldn't pass a newsstand without seeing their faces on the covers of a dozen newspapers and magazines. You couldn't turn on the TV without hearing about them. On the streets, on the set, along the beach—every conversation seemed to be about them. The American Prince and his Beautiful Princess. Gone.

Even in the privacy of my hotel room, late at night, with the lights off and nothing to disturb me, there was no escaping her. I kept reviewing our life together. The first time I saw her at Joe's Café. Four straight days on my red futon. The day she came to see me at the Paramount Hotel. The visits to Naugatuck. I only remembered the good things, and there were many of them, but at the end of the week I remembered one of the bad things, and it was the very worst of all. It was that weekend in Seattle, when I'd flown up for Gordon's mother's funeral. Carolyn had asked me for help, and I had said no.

I found myself wondering what would have happened if I had said yes. Would Carolyn have left John Jr.? Would she be alive today? Would we be together? Would we be happy?

But of course I hadn't said yes. I'd said no. That was my final word to Carolyn, and I could never take it back.

10.

Life After Carolyn

One word
Frees us of all the weight and pain of life:
That word is love.
　　　　—Sophocles, *Oedipus at Colonus*

When the news began to die down, I flew back to Los Angeles and moved Joy out of her place and into my apartment, then took her to Connecticut to meet my family. Everyone adored her and her little belly. The pull of fatherhood grew stronger with each passing day.

We got back to our lives and our demons. Well, *my* demons, mostly. I was still cautious, still distant, still keeping Joy at arm's length. I was protecting myself, and I was doing it at her expense. At a time when she really needed me, I was emotionally removed.

During the last trimester, I was back in Hawaii working, and managed to fly home only twice. But in October I was back for the birth of our little boy, my son, Jesse. I can't even begin to describe the feeling. This little creature, a living, mewling being that I could balance in the palm of my hand—was *ours*. We had created him together.

Jesse's birth went a long way in helping us through our troubles. Fatherhood is humbling. Suddenly you are not the center of the universe, and it's a *good* thing. There's a little person there, depending on you, looking to you for his very survival, and the responsibility is both overwhelming and overwhelmingly satisfying.

Joy and Jesse came to stay with me in Hawaii during the latter part of the season, and I was such a total *dad* that I know I was driving people crazy He wasn't speaking yet of course—he wasn't even two months old—but I'd run around all day saying things like: "He said *baba* this morning! Just like that, *baba*, clear as a bell. My son's a genius!"

When the season was over, we went to Connecticut to introduce Jesse to my family. Everyone was bowled over and madly in love with him, and they even fought over the privilege of changing his diapers.

Then, before we knew it, we were back in L.A. Joy, Jesse, and I. A family that wasn't really a family. Joy was the mother of my child, but I wasn't marrying her. Where did that leave her? Or where did that leave Jesse, for that matter? What did the future hold? What could she expect?

I didn't have any answers, and, as usual, I lost myself in my work. I didn't want to deal with anything that caused me pain. I loved Joy, but I still lacked the courage to act on my feelings. So of course everything deteriorated. We fought and fought some more, and eventually the fighting got so ugly that she moved out.

It was the strangest feeling. My son and the mother of my son were gone. I was alone in my place, moving from room to room like an unhappy ghost.

Then the lawyers got into the mix. Support payments, visitation schedules, medical expenses. It was a nightmare, financially and emotionally.

Then my life got even weirder. I arrived home one day to find a mysterious letter from a man I'd never met. It had been forwarded to me by the Wilhelmina agency, which hadn't represented me in several years. The man said he had once worked for John F. Kennedy Jr. at *George*. He had something for me, something important, and he wondered if I'd be good enough to call.

There was a number on the bottom of the page, and I called it and left a message. Within an hour, he returned the call. He repeated that he had worked for *George,* then went on to say that he had been at a party at John and Carolyn's apartment, shortly before the plane crash, and that Carolyn had given him something for me. He was oddly vague, and I found the whole thing a little irritating, but of course I was very curious.

"What?" I said. "What did she give you?"

"You know," he said, still trying to avoid a direct answer. "Pictures. And some cuff links."

"Pictures? Cuff links?"

"Please," he said. "I'll explain everything. I'm coming out to L.A. next month. Can I buy you lunch?"

So of course I met him for lunch. What would you have done? He was staying at a hotel in Marina del Rey. I went over, and we met in the lobby. He seemed like a relatively normal guy—I'll call him Alan—and he led the way to the lobby restaurant. We sat down and ordered, and I urged him to tell me the story. I still didn't know anything about this guy. For all I knew, he was just an obsessed fan, and he was making up this whole business about the pictures and the cuff links. But no, he said, it was true: all of it was true. And he began to tell me his strange story. He was at a party at John and Carolyn's loft, in Tribeca, he said, in late May 1999. John and Carolyn got into an argument. Somehow, my name came up. Alan thought John was jealous, and that he was throwing me in her face to shame her or piss her off, and Carolyn stormed into the other room.

Alan didn't know what to do. He followed Carolyn and asked if he could help, but she said she was fine. She was trying to make light of it, but she was still upset. So Alan, curious, asked her who John had been referring to, and she told him: "Michael. Michael Bergin. We dated a long time ago. He's on *Baywatch* now."

Alan had seen a few episodes of *Baywatch,* but he didn't know which one I was, and Carolyn offered to show him. He said she took him into the bedroom, went into her closet, and came back with a big box of stuff. It was filled with pictures of me. Tearsheets mostly. Dozens and dozens of them. All of these modeling gigs I'd done over the years, along with a few press clippings. Some of the items were loose, but others had been lovingly organized in large albums. That was the word Alan used: *lovingly*. Then she reached past the clips and photographs and showed him a little felt box. She opened it. A pair of monogrammed cuff links were inside.

"Carolyn said she had bought them for you as a Father's Day gift," Alan said.

I felt the hair literally standing up on the back of my neck. "What did you just say?" I asked.

"Just what Carolyn said. That she had bought you the cuff links for Father's Day."

It sounded crazy. I began to wonder about this guy. Then I realized that I'd told Gordon about Joy's pregnancy, and that he had probably shared the news with her.

"Are you sure that's what she said?" I asked.

"Yes," Alan said.

"What else did she say?"

"Not much," Alan said. "Because while we were standing there, looking at this stuff, the door burst open and John stormed in. And when he walked over and saw all those tearsheets he went ballistic. He just said, 'What the fuck is all this?! This is great, Carolyn! Fucking great!' And he stormed back out. Carolyn gave me the whole box—she literally pressed it into my hands, looking horrified—and said, 'Here! Take this. Please! Please take this!' And then she ran out after John."

"And then?"

"Nothing. Then the party broke up, because it looked like she had chased John out into the street, and everyone went home. And I took the whole box with me."

"So where is it?" I said. At this point, I could barely contain myself. He signed the check, we went up to his room, and he went and got the box. And sure enough, it was just as he said. Dozens and dozens of tearsheets, some of them stacked in no apparent order, others neatly arranged in albums. And then the smaller box. He took it out and showed me the cuff links. The initials MB were etched on the surface. I got chills all over again.

"See how the letters are a little crooked on this one?" Alan said. "Maybe that's why she didn't send them right away. Maybe she was going to have them redone."

"I've got to go," I said, upset. "I have to get back."

"I'll walk you out," he said. He could see that I was badly shaken up. "Here. All this is yours. Please take it."

"You think I should?" I asked.

"Of course," he said. "That's why I brought it. I brought it for you."

We went downstairs, and the valet went to get my car. As we were waiting, Alan did a very strange thing. He asked if he could have his picture taken with me. I said sure: I wasn't even thinking at that point. He stopped a passer-by and asked him to take our picture. The man took the picture and then the valet arrived with my car. I shook Alan's hand, thanked him, and left.

I was pretty freaked. I didn't know what to believe. Was Alan for real? Or was he just some psycho fan who had concocted that entire story so he could meet me?

The world is a crazy place. And a little scary. At the end of the day, all you've really got is your family.

I called Joy. I told her I wanted to try to make it work. Could we stop all the craziness? Could we try to make peace?

She was all for it. And we tried.

But it didn't happen overnight.

I worked and she worked and we worked on raising our son together.

Occasionally, reporters would call for some comment about my life with Carolyn, and I always declined politely. They always had an angle, of course: It had been a year since her death. It would have been her birthday. This was the day President Kennedy was shot and killed in Dallas. It was madness. Anything to rehash the tragic past.

One day I got a call from Sarah Ramaker, my manager at the time. She told me she had just heard from Ed Klein, a writer. Klein was doing an article for *Parade* magazine, and he wanted to ask me a few questions about my acting career and fitness regimen. I told her to go ahead and give him my cell phone number, and Klein called the next day. He asked me about *Wolves of Wall Street*, a feature I'd done with Eric Roberts, and about *Passions*, a daytime soap in which I played the heavy, then he suddenly changed the subject and began to ask about Carolyn. I was used to this—everyone always asked about Carolyn—and I told him that she was a terrific woman, that we'd been very close, but that I really had nothing more to say about her. He didn't seem thrilled by my response. He thanked me for my time, rather abruptly, and got off the phone.

A week later, he called again. This time he had a different story. He was doing a book on the Kennedys, not an article for *Parade,* and he wanted to know more about my relationship with Carolyn. He noted, however, that he already knew a great deal about the relation- ship. One reliable source, unnamed of course, had told him that Carolyn and I had been having an affair, that she had violent mood swings, and that she abused drugs. I was stunned. I had a simple choice: I could either hang up, or I could try to correct his miscon- ceptions and set the record straight. I opted for the latter.

I told Klein that his source was wrong—dead wrong. I told him that Carolyn had been a wonderful woman, that she had been the best friend I'd ever had, and that I never would have survived New York without her. I went on at some length, saying nothing but the nicest things about Carolyn, and meaning every last word. But this didn't seem to be what Klein wanted to hear. He kept pushing me on the alleged drug use and the mood swings and the craziness. I told him that there hadn't been any drug use to speak of. I said that in the entire time I'd known Carolyn, there were only two occasions when I actually saw her near cocaine. She did a line or two, yes, but I don't think she enjoyed it. My impression was that she did it to play along, to be part of the group.

As for mood swings, I told him there hadn't been any. But I did tell him about the night I went to Nell's, with Nicole, and Carolyn had attacked me in full view of everyone at the bar, then followed me home. I told him about the big candles and the broken window and gouged plaster and the chunk she'd taken out of the wooden floor. And I told him about the way she had chased me down the street. "She was pretty pissed off," I told him. "But she had good reason to be."

Then he came right out and asked me again, point-blank, if I'd had an affair with her. "No," I said, trying to protect her. "As far as I know, she was happily married."

Klein thanked me and said good-bye. We had spent maybe twenty minutes on the phone. I forgot about the brief conversation and went on with my life.

Joy and I were together again, in love, better than ever, and working hard at being a real family. *Baywatch* ended in 2001, but in 2002 it was resuscitated as a TV movie: *Baywatch: Hawaiian Wedding*.

In July 2003, we took Jesse to Connecticut. While we were there, *The Kennedy Curse* hit the stores and became an instant bestseller. I realized that the author was the same Ed Klein who had interviewed me the previous year.

Suddenly, the shit hit the fan. I had gone on at length about the good Carolyn, the loving Carolyn, but Klein had emphasized the story about Nicole, and it sounded as if I was saying that Carolyn had been explosive.

I heard my name on TV talk shows. I was being vilified as the bitter ex-boyfriend. I was described as the guy who didn't get the girl. I was the other man.

For years I had said nothing. *Not a single word.* Then in an attempt to protect Carolyn I made the mistake of talking to one writer, for twenty minutes, and in the eyes of the entire world was suddenly a louse and a bastard.

On July 2, the *New York Post* ran its usual banner headline: KENNEDY "BETRAYAL" was splashed across the front page. Inside, the article described me as JFK Jr.'s rival in love, and claimed that I still carried a torch for the Queen of Camelot. It said I had proposed to Carolyn on two occasions, and had been rebuffed both times. The story was all wrong, but it had a *ring* of truth. I guess that's why people believe that stuff.

It was terrible. I was back East with Joy and my son and my family, and everywhere I turned I was being treated with scorn and disgust. The whole world was standing in judgment of me, and they didn't know anything about me. They didn't know the real story.

To say it cast a pall over my visit home is to grossly understate the case. I was devastated. Joy was devastated. My own grandmother would answer the phone to find reporters on the other end, looking for me, asking her what she knew about this, how she felt about her grandson. It was beyond embarrassing. It was deeply painful.

When we got back to Los Angeles, it was more of the same. Paparazzi waiting for me at my house, the phone ringing off the hook, the tabloids calling and offering me obscene amounts of money.

I turned down every offer.

I woke up one morning to find somebody behind my place, going through the trash. On another occasion, I discovered that my mailbox had been vandalized.

I started getting hate mail. Here's an example of one of the few letters I can print:

"Congratulations on all the publicity you are getting this past month concerning the death of Carolyn and JFK and the new book by Klien [sic]. What a great way to get your name back into the entertainment community.

It really sucks that you have to do this. But what else can you do? You can't get a job doing anything but *Baywatch* and you don't even look good anymore. Gee, I wonder why? Maybe you're into the drug scene also? Times are bad and you are the typical actor that is just plain lazy and road [sic] the gravy train. Now the gravy train has pulled into the station and has stopped. What's next?"

I was shattered. I felt like defending myself, but I didn't know where to begin, and I certainly didn't trust the press. I hadn't read Klein's book because I didn't want to see what he'd done to Carolyn, but I finally caved in and read it. I felt like crying. He couldn't have been more unflattering, or more wrong.

I wanted to set the record straight. Not only for Carolyn, but for me. And for Joy. I never thought I would find someone I loved as much as I had loved Carolyn, but I did. Joy had stood by me, never wavering, and she was an amazing partner and mother. I was a lucky man.

I felt that the truth needed to be told, and I decided that this book was the way I wanted to tell it.

I was terrified at first. I had to relive my entire life, with the emphasis on my relationship with Carolyn. I felt like I was in therapy. It was hard on me, and it was hard on Joy. But I told Joy I had to do this. If I could get the story out there, the *true* story, we could get on with our lives.

I would face my mistakes. I hoped the truth would set me free.

When I told my friends and family about the book, not all of them were supportive. Even my parents had doubts. They thought I intended to write a tawdry tell-all memoir. People would find it shameless, they said. Carolyn was a beautiful young woman whose life had been cut tragically short, and I'd be vilified by the critics because she was dead and gone and unable to defend herself.

"You don't understand," I said. "She won't have to defend herself. That's why I'm writing the book. *I'm* defending her."

Even as I began to write, the lies kept coming. But they were no longer run-of-the-mill lies about drug use and mood swings and jealous rages. Now the nature of the lies themselves had changed. Now the lies were about John and Carolyn's fairy-tale marriage. Yes, the reporters said, they'd had some problems. Don't we all have problems? It was hard for Carolyn to adjust to the glare of publicity. Hard for her to leave her job and adjust to the new reality of being simply Mrs. John F. Kennedy Jr. But she had adjusted admirably. And the future never looked brighter. And she and John Jr. were happier than ever, talking about having children and building a dream home in Connecticut, far from the madness of New York.

But I'm not so sure. If they were so happy, why had Carolyn asked me to save her when we saw each other in Seattle? Why did she seem so miserable and act like she wanted out of her marriage? Why had she told me she loved me?

On the other hand, it's possible she *was* happy. Fourteen months had elapsed between our fateful meeting in Seattle and her untimely death in July 1999. Maybe her life *had* turned around. Maybe she and John really had found their way back.

I know, I know. Alan had arrived in L.A. with those tearsheets and the monogrammed cuff links, and he'd told me all about that big fight at their loft. John had burst out of the apartment in a huff, and Carolyn had chased him into the street. And if he was to be believed, this was barely two months before they died. But was it true? And even it if was true, what did it prove? That they fought? I fight with Joy from time to time. But I still love her.

I don't honestly know what happened in the last fourteen months of Carolyn's life, and I don't think it's my business to try to guess. I'll never know. But I hope good things happened. I hope John and Carolyn really did find their way. I hope Carolyn found the love and happiness she deserved.

Carolyn was just a human being like any other. And, like the rest of us, she made mistakes. The mistakes were sometimes ugly, and sometimes downright horrible, but they were always human. Yes, Carolyn had her demons. Like the rest of us. And like the rest of us, she struggled.

I too have my own demons, and I have struggled. I've made my own mistakes, and I'm not proud of them, and I'm sure I will make more mistakes in years to come. I too am a human being, with plenty of my own flaws, maybe more than the average man. I don't know. All I know is that I work on myself every day, and that every day I try to make a little progress. And on those days when I don't feel I'm making any headway, when I feel as if I'm slipping and falling even further behind, I try even harder.

In closing, I will tell you this from the bottom of my heart: if Carolyn's up there, looking down on us, I know she'd be okay with this book. *More* than okay. I think she'd welcome it. Because it's the truth. This is what really happened, and this is the way it happened.

I once loved Carolyn, and she still holds a special place in my heart. I consider myself lucky to have known her. My life is richer because of her.

But life does go on.

I am at peace with myself and at peace with what I've written here.

I have a life to lead.

And life is a blessing.

I didn't always know that, but I know it now.

ACKNOWLEDGMENTS

Mom, Dad: Thank you for being the best parents a man could wish for. I've always tried to make you proud, and I hope I never fail you.

Ron Jr., Tina, Jessica: You were always there for me. I will never forget it.

Angie and Margaret, my two wonderful grandmothers: I love you and miss you every day.

Jason Brooks: For your wisdom and guidance.

Jonathan Silverman, Craig Ley, Lori Heuring, Michael Marchand: Cheers. I cherish our friendship.

Laura Lightbody and Jennifer Norton Pace: Thank you for making a difference.

Tommy, B.J., Ed, Bob, Scott, Mike S., Mike W., Todd, Shane, Jeff, Mark G., Mark H., Sonny, John L., Rudy, Randy, and the whole Naugatuck gang: For the memories and your continuing friendship.

Patrick Meyler and Robert Tribe: Thanks for the little things.

Stuart Rogers Acting Studio: Thanks for improving the skills.

Stephanie Simon: For your friendship, advice, and professional guidance.

Matt Maletta: Thanks for your counsel. Brian Edwards: Thanks for time and efforts.

Judith Regan: You were interested only in the truth, and you listened to me. Thank you for letting me tell my story, my way.

Brian Saliba: For your keen eye and fine editing skills.

P. Lo: For being a better therapist than my therapist, and for helping me shape these memories into a book.

Anna, Dick, Lisa: I share your loss.

Gordon: My biggest fan. I miss you, pal.

Carolyn: You will never be forgotten.

Rest in peace.